I Brake for Butterflies

Finding Divinity in All That Is . . .

JUDITH M. CAMPBELL

Published by

 GENERAL STORE
GSPH PUBLISHING HOUSE

499 O'Brien Road, Box 415
Renfrew, Ontario, Canada K7V 4A6
Telephone (613) 432-7697 or 1-800-465-6072

ISBN 1-897113-45-5
Printed and bound in Canada

Formatting and printing by Custom Printers of Renfrew Ltd.
Front Cover photo: © Photographer: Anita Patterson Peppers
Agency: Dreamstime.com
Back Cover Butterfly Image: © Artist: Angie McLaughlin
wallcandycreations.com

General Store Publishing House
Renfrew, Ontario, Canada

Library and Archives Canada Cataloguing in Publication

Campbell, Judith M. (Judith Marian), 1945-
        I brake for butterflies : finding divinity in all that is / Judith M.
Campbell.

Includes bibliographical references.
ISBN 1-897113-45-5

        1. Spiritual life. 2. Self-realization. I. Title.

BL624.C335 2006   204'.4   C2006-902855-9

God outsmarted the scientists when "He" created the world. He made it virtually impossible to prove His existence . . . except through belief!

. . . thanks be to God!

Contents

Introduction

The first thing I want to say to you as you begin to read this book is that it has nothing to do with butterflies—at least, not directly! I have chosen this title because it symbolically represents what I am trying to say about the divinity of life.

When we come into an awareness of the divine nature that is throughout the universe, we *do* brake for the butterflies that come into our path—or we *want to*. It saddens us to see animals that are struck on the highways or to think about the animals we don't see that meet their death in unnatural ways. And we are filled with gratitude for the gifts that are given so freely to us throughout nature—gifts such as the beauty and colour found in a butterfly's delicate yet sturdy wings.

The butterfly is a symbol of transformation, however we may wish to view this meaning. It represents the final and most important stage of the progression in the life of a simple caterpillar. As *we* progress along life's journey, we also go through many transitions. We grow and mature into new ways of being.

Specifically, the butterfly beautifully symbolizes the transformation that takes place within us as we begin to connect with the divinity of our spirit. It highlights the awe and beauty of this stage. But, rather than seeing the butterfly as symbolizing the death of the physical body, instead consider the butterfly as representing an exciting stage in the evolution of the spirit and soul within the human body.

After all, when the Monarch gets her wings, it represents the beginning of the rest of her life. If emerging in the early fall, she has a huge journey to make from the northern U.S. and Canada to the Gulf of Mexico coast to escape the cold of winter. She needs her wings to make this incredible journey. And only after she reaches her destination is she ready to fulfill her purpose within creation—to ensure the continuation of her species. Even then, she attempts a return trip back to the place of her birth.

The human equivalent of this stage in our lives is where we recognize our spirit as a light-giving force in our body, capable of transforming us as we learn to release control over every aspect of our lives and surrender to a new way of being that is completely guided by our spirit. This is where we find life's meaning. Finally, our soul's voice has been heard. From this point on, we begin to do the real work of our life. We are released from the prison of our mind. We are free. Like the butterfly, our transformation has allowed us to crack open our chrysalis and emerge as the beautiful spiritual beings we are.

Regrettably, far too many humans never reach this stage of their lives, not because of illness or untimely death, but because of their lack of awareness of themselves as spiritual beings. Ironically, illness is often the catalyst to achieving this sense of awareness. And terminal illness can catapult its "victim" into a complete understanding of himself as spirit and help him to finish his journey on earth with feelings of wholeness, completion, and peace.

As you read through this book, I invite you to consider at what stage you are in your own transition towards becoming a butterfly or in making your journey on earth as a butterfly.

You will notice that I use both the words spirit and soul throughout this book. According to dictionary definitions, these words are synonyms for each other. However, in my opinion there are some subtle differences. Whereas "spirit" is universal, in my view "soul" is personal. But just as it takes both the yolk and the albumin to make an egg, so, too, are both spirit and soul found together in one unit. I have provided a detailed explanation of this in Chapter Six, under the heading "The Duality of Spirit."

By way of introduction to the book's subtitle, *Finding Divinity in All That Is*, I am including a poem that has been the genesis of this book. It was written during the late summer of 2004 while I was on a weekend retreat at Galilee Centre, in Arnprior, Ontario.

It is significant that the words of this poem came to me in a location that is literally a stone's throw from my place of birth. Galilee is my favourite place to facilitate workshops and retreats and to attend the same given by others. Its buildings are set within an oasis of ancient, giant pine trees on the banks of the Ottawa River, several miles upstream from the city of Ottawa, Canada's capital. It is a sacred place to go to find nourishment for the body, mind, and spirit, and healing of the soul. Every time I go to Galilee, I either find healing within myself or I am privileged to witness it in others.

On this particular weekend, early on the first day, I experienced a moment of insight in which I was suddenly overcome by the sensation that I was hundreds of years old! I can't explain how this feeling arose. It just did. It lasted only seconds, but its effects are with me still.

In telling a spiritually minded new friend—an octogenarian—about my experience afterwards, her comment to me was, "You mean thousands of years old, don't you, dear?—billions, even." In this brief, mind-altering experience, I had apparently glimpsed eternity! The words of the poem came to me following this experience.

I am in the mists of time.
I am in the silent sounds of waters.
I am in the thunderous sounds of
oceans.
I am in the gentle breezes and
the tumultuous hurricanes.
I am in *all that is*.

I find myself only as I awaken
to this level of consciousness:
this level of consciousness that
acknowledges,
this level of consciousness that knows,
this level of consciousness that
understands
that I am in all that is.

Here, healing is in the past.
Healing is in the present.
Healing will be in the future.
For there will be times when I will
forget my past;
there will be times when I will forget
that I am in all that is.

And then, something within this grand
spectrum of nature
will guide me back to the place
inside of me that remembers
when time began,
and I will once again *know*
that I am in all that is.

We are in all that is.
We are each a part of Divinity.
We are in our friends
and in our enemies.
We are in all that is.

I am in *you* and *you* are in *me!*
Together we engage this journey.
Together we teach each other,
reflect each other's
imperfections and perfections
as we strive for harmony . . .
as we try to remember that
we are in all that is.

Together, we answer the call to return
to the Source,
the Source of all that is;
for it is here that we find
the peace we search for,
the joy waiting to be expressed,
the love available to all.

We are in the mists of time.
We are in the silent sounds of waters.
We are in the thunderous sounds of
oceans.
We are in the gentle breezes
and in the tumultuous hurricanes
We are in all that is!

As a result of those brief seconds in time, I have been able to step outside my physical reality to view humanity in a much more expansive way. And in the process, I have stumbled upon what is known as "the divinity of man."

This book, then, addresses the subject of divinity under the subtitle of *Finding Divinity in All That Is*. For I have come to understand that these two subject areas are intrinsically related. To understand that divinity exists within humanity is to come into an understanding that divinity also exists in all that is— including butterflies!

As in all my writing, I write only when I feel inspired to write. In so doing, I give full credit to a force that is working through me as I write. This is part of my own divinity, which gently guides me to work in this way. And when I do work in this way, I know I have access to "intelligence" that is made available to me in a spiritual sense. Some would simply call this *creativity*.

This book addresses a number of different topics that I think you will consider relevant in today's world of change and uncertainty. It offers an approach to living your *physical* reality with a renewed sense of dignity and purposeful contribution.

Here, you can get more enjoyment out of life and live your life fully and, in the process, leave the world a better place for *your* having been here.

And it is more than this. To touch upon the subject of human divinity is to become knowledgeable about *one's own divinity*. This first requires awareness, and then a willingness to view one's life and the meaning of life in broadened terms.

In the words of a former teacher, Leah Smith: "You must be willing to suspend your disbeliefs . . . as well as your beliefs [i.e. when you are confronted with new ideas] and consider *what might be* as opposed to what isn't."

Author Michael J. Roads describes how he felt disturbed following the completion of his book about the oneness of humanity. He says, "I have learned that our view of life has become so conditioned and limited that we [are able to] see no more than a distortion of what *Is*."[1]

His publishers, Hal and Linda Kramer, go on to say in their inscribed mission statement: "The books we publish are our contribution to an emerging world based on . . . an affirmation of the human spirit . . . and on the certainty that all humanity is connected."[2]

I Brake for Butterflies takes this view a step further and suggests that not only is all of humanity connected, all that has life is connected; all that is within creation is connected!

In fact, all that is within creation is a container for divinity because of this connection.

---

[1] Michael J. Roads, *Journey into Oneness: A Spiritual Odyssey* (Tiburon, Calif.: H.J. Kramer Inc, 1994), p 225.

[2] Ibid, p. vi.

Frustrated churchgoers may have deemed "the divinity of man" a concept only relevant to spiritual leaders, some of whom have been declared *saints* following an extensive post-mortem process that examined their lives and determined their *worthiness* of the honour. It is exactly this kind of process that serves to separate us from the idea of ever being a vessel for divinity ourselves! It sets divinity up on such a high pedestal, we perceive that *only* saints and esteemed religious leaders may ever experience it.

It is only through the humble recognition and understanding that we are capable of having divinity revealed within us that we are able to make the transition from living a purely physical existence to being able to attain and sustain a sense of who we *really* are—spiritual beings living within a physical dimension, part of *all that is*.

And from this place of inner knowing, we move more intently to the place in which we outwardly know ourselves as someone who possesses a spirit and soul that is connected to the God-force or *Source* of creation.

Here, we begin to truly understand that we contain the energy of divinity within our own being! It is not only outside of us. It is also within us. *It is our connector to all else in the universe!* It is what allows mankind to see the commonality amongst *all* living creatures. It is what *could* allow peace to be found within mankind, and which one day . . . *may*.

One of the ways to make the connection with one's inner divinity is through an appreciation of the incredible gift of music that has been given to us by composers like Handel, Beethoven, Mendelssohn, Mozart, Holst, Willan, and Rutter! Their Christian music transcends the human inadequacies of traditional Biblical interpretation, which often tends to create confusion in the minds of people in modern society.

This music has clearly been divinely inspired. The composers, through their talents and abilities, have served as vehicles for the divine quality of the music to flow through them and be captured on manuscripts for the benefit of all. The *Messiah* was written in only three weeks, for example. Music of this quality allows its listeners to *touch their own spirit* as they listen to words from religious scripture.

Inspirational music of this calibre requires no verbal interpretation to be understood. It is simply enjoyed in the fullness of its original beauty—its purity intact. It allows for the unification of religious values and human spiritual understanding; it provides the ability to find a new way of worshipping a universal God-force that is found in *all that is*.

Dr. Randall McClellan, a leading American authority on the healing properties of music, in speaking of the importance of music in religious and national rituals, states that music has a more powerful effect than words alone, rendering musicians with the potential for greater influence over others than most political leaders or national ideologies.[3]

And for some, inspirational music can actually melt away the chaos of confusion of religious teachings they received as a child. It offers a unique method for individuals to find their own way to the true meaning of a religious value system they can fully endorse.

Human spirituality need not be a mystery. It contains the same energy quality as that which is contained throughout living creation. It is the energy of the universal life force—the Source of Creation. Its essence is divinity. Its context is timeless. It endures all things. The words of the poem above convey this quite dynamically. It is with us throughout our earthly existence and it is with us as we make our final transition from our earthly body at the time of our physical death and continues to remain with us forever—for it *is* "us."

We lose touch with our spiritual identity when we focus on the physical aspect of our being. Too much attention focused on the physical dimension makes us forget our spiritual identity and creates a distinct imbalance in the way we live our lives.

It often takes a life crisis to bring us back to examine the question of whether there is more to life than what we see. To become reacquainted with ourselves as "spirit" opens us to a completely new understanding of balanced living.

To subscribe to this way of viewing life through a spiritual lens is to release childhood imagery of an all-powerful, external God and to soften into a new view of an all-powerful, *loving energy* (of God) that resides within each of us.

"As long as theologians make a childish idea of God," says author and philosopher Edouard Schuré, "and as long as men of science simply ignore or deny *Him*, the moral, social and religious unity of our planet will be only a pious desire or a postulate of religion and science, which are powerless to effect it."[4]

If we can feel the loving energy of God—of our own Buddha nature—*flowing through us*, then we can most assuredly find this loving energy outside of us in others. And in time, we will find this loving energy in *all that is*. And in this . . . there would be unity within our planet!

And now, with this peek into what is to follow, may I just say *thank you* for your intention to read this book, and may you find something within it that speaks to you that you are yearning to hear at this time in your life.

Namaste! (I bow to the divine in you.)

Judith

---

[3] Randall McClellan, Ph.D., *The Healing Forces of Music: History Theory and Practice*, (Warwick, New York: Amity House, Inc., 1988), p 151.

[4] Edouard Schuré, *The Great Initiates: A Study of the Secret History of Religions* (San Francisco: Harper & Row Publishers, 1961), p. 172. (Originally published in France in 1889.)

ONE

GOING MORE DEEPLY INTO SPIRITUALITY

*In the circle of life, we all come from Divine love. We all return to Divine love.
Divine love is cleansing, purifying, restoring, and redeeming.
Divine love is in all that is.*

What is spirituality? How does one experience spirituality? Can *everyone* experience spirituality—his own, or that of someone else?

My own immersion into spirituality began after someone told me I was living the majority of my life "in the physical" and that as a result of this my life had become very imbalanced. What did she mean by "living my life in the physical"? I asked.

"You go about each day doing all the things that have become your way of life without any thought given to another way of living," she said; "a spiritual way of living."

"But how can I live spiritually?" I asked her, the thought never having crossed my mind before.

"By learning to look at yourself as a spiritual being," she responded easily and simply. And then she suggested three books for me to read to help me embark on my own spiritual quest.

Those three books were the beginning of what would become a library of books on the subject of spirituality and a journey that I have discovered has no end. I felt as though I had opened an invisible door into an entirely new and exciting world—a world where I felt completely comfortable and whole, at peace, and most of all, *at home*. I was about to discover that this was the first of many doors I would open as I pursued a journey with my spirit.

And as I am now realizing, the doors continue to be there awaiting our progression and readiness to open them, each one taking us more deeply than the last into the subject of spirituality. Just as our physical growth and our mental understanding pass through many stages to reach maturity, so, too, does our relationship with our spirit.

And just as our libraries and institutions of higher learning are filled with books of knowledge attesting to the discoveries made by brilliant minds worldwide, so, too, is the capacity for deeper and deeper insight and understanding of the infinite subject of spirituality.

Spirituality begins with an immersion in the understanding that there is more to the human being than just the body and the mind. And in our early stages of getting to know our spirit, we come to a full realization that *it is who we actually are.*

Further, we begin to understand that our spirit is something intangible that will outlive the physical body in which it resides. From this basic comprehension, spirituality moves us into a deeper appreciation for those things that allow us to focus on a deeper meaning of life.

Acknowledging our spirituality puts us in touch with the concept of a God-force or Buddha-nature that exists throughout all creation, in a nonreligious and quite meaningful way. It provides us with a respect for all humanity and for all of creation. It therefore frees us from egocentric thinking and behaviours. It allows us to become responsible human beings who understand that there are consequences for every action we take in life. It teaches us that we are responsible for how we deal with the reality of our life's circumstances.

It is in *how* we do this that we become the creators of our own reality. We can choose to assume the role of victim because of what has happened to us, or we may rise above this completely self-inflicted dysfunctional way of being, and begin the process of fixing what went wrong. It is here that awareness of ourselves as spirit becomes extremely valuable in strengthening us and helping us to recover and heal.

The realization of oneself as spirit is most empowering yet humbling at the same time. For as we learn to work and live within a new set of guidelines that are spiritually grounded, we also learn to surrender to a new way of living, unleashing the perception that we have full control over the direction our life will take. *It is here that the physical and spiritual worlds meet.* Our awareness now opens us to a new sense of being, completely guided by spirit in all that we do in our physical world.

It takes time to reach this stage of spiritual maturity. When we progress to this stage, however, we can begin to conceptualize ourselves as being divinely connected to the positive forces of the universe, to the *God-force* of creation.

Naturally, this causes us to expand our logical thinking on the meaning and mystery of God. *He* is no longer the entity that we may have created in our minds at some point in our early childhood. Instead, we begin to imagine "God" quite differently as something palpable and universal that we can feel and possibly even hear as we live within a state of awareness of ourselves as spiritual beings.

Eventually, our perception of a universal God moves our thinking towards that of a *life-force* comprised of energy—*divine spiritual energy*—that is throughout the entire universe. And caught up in this divine spiritual energy is humanity and all within creation that has life. We might even drop the term "*God*" from our vocabulary and substitute the word "*Spirit*" to convey the meaning of this new perception and understanding we have of God.

And from this, we begin to develop new attitudes about life. We develop a new respect for *all* of life and for all of life's forms. We develop new attitudes about *our* life, about our purpose in life, and about how our life relates to others' lives.

As part of this process of spiritual awakening and development, we begin to heal old ways and outdated belief systems and attitudes. These were the belief systems that kept us stuck in traditional thinking and traditional beliefs—"man-made" beliefs.

As we free ourselves of these old ways, beliefs, and attitudes, we actually feel ourselves getting lighter, as though a burden has been lifted from our bodies and from our minds. This is very much a part of our own healing and release that begins—naturally—when we immerse ourselves in our own spirituality.

We begin to experience clarity in our understanding. Even our physical vision appears clearer. Visual clarity allows us to appreciate the beauty that surrounds us that may previously have been hidden from our view. We are reminded of the talents we possess and we find ourselves wanting to use them (again).

We begin to take time to be grateful for the blessings we have in our life. Suddenly, we realize just how many blessings we *do* have, and we can count more with each new day.

We begin to honour and respect our bodies and to feel love for the spiritual aspect of ourselves. And eventually, we also feel love for our physical and mental aspects as well. With this complete feeling of love comes compassion for ourselves.

This means that all former self-criticism that may have plagued our minds from an early age is replaced with love. We release all of the negativity we have held within our being about ourselves and replace it with love. In other words, we release all our *negative energy* and replace it with the *positive energy of love*. Thus, we have *healed* this aspect of ourselves.

From this perspective, we are less critical of others, also. In fact, we begin to develop a sense of compassion for those people in our lives whom we may formerly have treated poorly or who have treated us poorly. It is this move towards compassion that allows us to begin to forgive and to seek forgiveness.

As a result of the release of negative energy from our being through the giving and receiving of forgiveness—negative energy that shows up in our behaviours, attitudes, and thinking—we are able to connect with the best part of people henceforth, and thus we are able to relate to them in more positive ways. In other words, we are able to find the good that is in each person rather than focusing on what we would have formerly viewed as flaws.

Eventually we don't even see the flaws. Criticism has been replaced by concern, compassion, or possibly even detachment. We are able to share more of ourselves because we have stopped focusing on what we previously perceived as flaws in ourselves also. We are truly able to love ourselves and to mirror our self-love to everyone.

This newfound freedom gives licence to others to experience the best part of *themselves* also when they are with us, and when this happens, the universal life-force (divinity) moves through us all. We *all* feel it. In the circle of life, we all come from Divine love. Divine love is cleansing, purifying, restoring, and redeeming. When the Divine spirit moves through us all, it provides healing for us all. It cleanses, purifies, restores, and redeems us. It connects us with the very best part of ourselves and of one another.

Spiritual Oneness

It is from this place of personal growth and spiritual maturity that we can move into a position of understanding the concept of *oneness* throughout humanity and all of creation. We come to fully appreciate that this sense of oneness is possible because of our spiritual similarity and that we are each part of a much greater spiritual opportunity within the universe. I say spiritual opportunity because although we all contain a spiritual similarity within us, we do not all open ourselves to the potential for oneness throughout creation and all that this means.

When we don't open ourselves to the spiritual opportunities that exist for us, it is like living our lives within only one windowless room of a house, never having explored the rest of the house or gone outside to see what awaits us there. And within this one room, we focus only on our physical being—on our basic needs that keep us alive and fuel an egocentric way of being.

When we share this room with like-minded people, we remain stuck within this physical place, unable to see the light that calls to us from the other side of the door. And eventually, it becomes too difficult even to find the door—*but it is always there, waiting to be opened.* And sometimes, it is opened for us through some force that is much greater than us, and we are gently guided out of the room where we have spent our lives thus far and into the light of day.

Or we may be blasted out through the door by personal tragedy, serious illness, the loss of our job, or some other life-changing event. And once opened, it is rare that we will ever want to go back into that room again—the room that never sees light.

It is through a spiritual energy connection with the universal life force—a greater power or God-force—that simple people like you and me can accomplish great things. It is the divine energy of the God-force working in us and through us that allows this to happen. And because of this higher spiritual energy connection to which we have opened ourselves, we are able to view all of life from a spiritual context, an ongoing spiritual context that has no end.

Learning to live a spiritually guided life demands that we maintain a complete awareness at all times of the spiritual dimension of our life. It teaches us to submit to a constant inner voice that guides us through every seemingly inconsequential activity and interchange with others.

We learn to respect and care for our physical body and mind, nourishing and exercising both in proper ways. And we discover that we need to nourish our spirit and soul also by immersing them in an environment and activities that are conducive to an inner sense of well-being.

The reward for the continual nourishment of your body, mind, spirit, and soul is a life that is filled with meaning—a life that feels like each new day is filled with purposeful living, wherein your mind is constantly challenged to submit to an inner voice as opposed to a rational, mindful dialogue.

Here, you will be drawn out of complacency as you become respectful of your own life and of all creation. You will feel a sense of being one with *all that is* while at the same time detached from the common problems of others—allowing others to find their own way through life—yet observant in a non-judgmental way, and willing to serve as a guide or mentor when needed.

Each new day presents opportunities for spiritual guidance to take place in the simplest of interchanges with others. And the more this happens, the more opportunities will come your way to give or receive guidance. The universe will continue to guide you through wherever it moves you into position to give or receive next. You will be given the energy, the confidence, the words and the ability to *do* and *say* and *be* all you are capable of, for your intention and your spiritual maturity will have moved you into the place of being that is completely spiritually connected and guided.

It is here you realize fully that your spiritual purpose is being revealed in every moment. And gradually, you will come into an awareness of the vastness of your spirit and the ageless aspect of the human spirit. It is this sense of agelessness that assures us that our spirit has been around since time began and that it is *filled* with wisdom and knowledge that provides us with the necessary information to live our humanity. Can you think about *yourself* in this way? How would it change your thoughts about yourself? Could it elevate you from the mundane, the depressed, or the lonely, and whisk you into an expanded outlook of your life and your reaction to your life?

Agelessness rocks the foundations of our thinking—in a good way! For once we have been able to fully comprehend ourselves as spirit, we can take the next giant step in our mental processing of spirituality to first consider, and then to realize, that our spirit has a history, a lineage.

Our history is all part of the spiritual aspect of ourselves. It is all contained within the spiritual dimension of our humanity, within our soul. And here is the awesome part: When did it come into being? The answer: *at the beginning of time.*

This, of course, suggests that the human spirit is part of *the Source of creation.* And as part of the Source of creation, the human spirit therefore takes on the dimension of *all that is* in life on this planet and in the universe.

In spirit is to be found every element of creation, of the life force itself, because we are part of the whole. We are part of the *entire* universe. This is the meaning of *oneness.* Oneness addresses the mystery of life through suggesting that at a very basic level—the level of spirit—humans and all that has life share a commonality. We all contain a similar divine spark of the excellence and perfection of creation.

As humans, we have within us at the level of spirit all aspects of creation, life, knowledge, and wisdom. On the physical level, we are able to tap into selective pathways to uncover this knowledge and wisdom through the use of our natural talents and the ensuing creativity that flows from their use.

Discovering this helps you to recognize yourself as spirit residing within a physical body. It is through the continual acknowledgement, nourishment, celebration, and gratitude of and for the wholeness of your life that you are able to maintain the awareness of yourself as spirit with unlimited access to the wisdom you hold within.

In our physical life, our spirit moulds itself into a unique way of being with an identity unlike other spiritual beings, yet with an identity that bears the divine energy quality of the God-force held by our spirit. This is the commonality we all share as human beings.

And within our spirit, we each hold a uniqueness that is our soul—the part of us that stores the history of our being and ensures our individuality. Within this physical existence we all have a body and mind. The body, mind, and spirit comprise the *holy trinity of our being.*

All of humanity contains the potential to experience the holy trinity as *personal wholeness* and *spiritual oneness* with God, the rest of humanity, and all that is. Acknowledging the capacity for oneness within humanity highlights the *sameness* of the peoples of the world and the *desperation* of war. It shows us how we have not evolved as a species on the planet.

On any given day, men, women, and children are being subjected to barbaric killings in countries all over the world. Whether caused by uncivilized political and military leadership, where democracy is viewed as a loss of control by the state and where the principles of Christianity hold no meaning; or whether the killings are isolated events in democratic and Christian countries, the evidence is present every night on the evening news and in the morning newspaper. In many ways, we have not progressed beyond the stage of larvae. Human dignity and respect are completely obfuscated within this spiritless reality.

There has never been a time in history when peacekeepers were more desperately needed. Peacekeeping police officers place themselves in harm's way every day to defend the public they serve. And the service performed by armed services personnel from peace-abiding countries is fast becoming one of the most meaningful and selfless jobs in the world. Young men and women are truly trying to make a difference—even giving their lives to uphold their beliefs in the human rights of oppressed peoples. The symbolic meaning of the death of Christ is realized again and again as peacekeepers and civilians die attempting to save the lives of others from the sins of mankind.

Meanwhile, back at home in these peace-abiding countries, we continue to fight with one another on a personal level. We continue to dishonour our parents, our brothers and sisters, our elders, our neighbours, our friends and associates, etc. We dishonour one another through disrespectful behaviours of one sort or another—all of which point to a failure to acknowledge that which we share in common within humanity, and as understood by seeing ourselves as spiritual beings.

As we go more deeply into our own spirituality, we begin to see not only the terrorist in terrorism, we catch a glimpse of *ourselves* as well. For until, as individuals, we are able to love and forgive each person in our personal lives whom we feel has hurt us in some way, we need to realize that we are also a threat to humanity. We are also guilty of perpetuating the negative energy that is fundamental to the fuelling of separation, the focus on differences, and the dysfunction that flows from these two jaded views of one's fellow man or woman.

Despite the spiritual commonality we all share—holding the energy of the divine spark of creation within our being—there will never truly be peace throughout the world until we, as physical beings, can respect one another, forgive one another, and most of all, love one another. The time has come to awaken from spiritless sleep and pay attention to the unseen as well as the seen, lest our blindness be our undoing—the world's undoing!

The time has come to recognize ourselves as the spiritual beings we are— part of the divinity of creation—without the perception of boundaries of colour, language, or creed separating us, or making us appear different, from one another.

The time has come to acknowledge ourselves as being free of *all* the encumbrances or obstacles we may have conjured in our physical minds about others. It is within this revitalized perception of reality that we can rise to our spiritually divine and human potential on the pinnacle of holiness, entrained in the mastery of the human spirit—one with the centre of the universe, one *with* all that is, one *in* all that is.

The time has come ....

This chapter is dedicated to the loving memory of
Jacob S. Fletcher
and his fellow military colleagues, who have given their young and dynamic lives to serve and protect the innocent peoples of Iraq and Afghanistan.

Greater love has no one than this,
that one lay down his life for his friends.

John 15:13

It is important to realize that the more deeply you go into the subject of spirituality, the more you will be able to resurrect your own spirit from the ashes of spiritual dis-connectors—things like egocentricity, selfish behaviour, jealousy, and so on. These are the human projections of mankind that make us forget our spirit and keep us in the lowest stages of our evolution. As we reconnect with our spirit, we rekindle our desire to give our spirit a prominent role in our life. Thus, we are taken through the stages of physical, mental, and emotional release and healing of those aspects of our being that have kept us separated from our true nature.

TWO

FINDING DIVINITY OUTSIDE "THE CHURCH"

Thou carriest within thee a sublime friend whom thou knowest not.
For God dwells in the inner part of every man, but few know how to find Him.

Bhagavad-Gita

In this chapter, it is my intention to help you to understand that divinity can be found anywhere and everywhere. We just need to learn how to find it and awaken to its daily presence in our lives.

Divinity can be found in our homes and workplaces, and in shopping centres, nursing homes, hospitals, restaurants, bookstores, and libraries. It may be found at the beach, on the golf course, or in the mountains. And yes, it may even be found in hockey arenas! It can be found *everywhere.* Divine qualities can be found in *all that is!*

I was struck by an incident recently while boarding a plane in Philadelphia. A young woman travelling with two small children had answered the early boarding call and preceded the rest of us several minutes earlier. But when I arrived at the alcove outside the aircraft, she was standing there, awaiting assistance from the airline personnel, holding her toddler in one arm, her other arm wrapped around the stroller, and her second child standing by her side clutching her skirt. The passengers hardly saw her there as they filed by her. Like myself, they probably assumed she was receiving help already, although none was apparent. Then the gentleman in front of me stopped to speak with her. I could hear his warm and friendly voice as he asked her if he could carry her stroller onto the plane for her. It both startled and impressed me, for I realized it had been quite some time since I'd been witness to a "good Samaritan" event.

I held the memory of this brief conversation in my mind long after witnessing it and I pondered the kindliness of it; the unwillingness to assume that help was on its way for her; the selflessness of the gesture: attending to someone else's needs before moving towards one's own comfort. And now, of course, I am writing about it. And although it was such a simple act that this man performed—an act that he probably didn't even think about once his offer was turned down—it struck me that it was the sort of thing we just don't see much any more.

People tend to be caught up in their own lives. Their minds are often running on overtime with thoughts, plans, and ideas, or with worries and the mental replaying of past events that could have gone better, and so on. Consequently, most of the travellers who passed by this woman hardly even saw her, or saw her as an impediment they had to move around as they boarded the aircraft.

But one individual *did* see her. His mind was clear and alert, and he offered her assistance. And in that special moment, as I stood by observing this scene, it felt *sacred*. Could this have been an example of divinity?

Divinity can be found anywhere. Divinity exposes itself through *selfless* behaviour. I should explain what I mean by "selfless." I mean that my own self-worth and my egocentric tendencies take a back seat to my immediate action. In other words, at the time when I react with selfless behaviour, I am not caught up in my own issues of neglect, loneliness, abuse, or a need to impress, etc. I am thinking only of someone else at that moment.

It is very difficult to behave in selfless ways when one's own life is fraught with problems. When one is suffering from the effects of neglect or abuse, the impact of these very negative and harmful qualities is such that many cannot rise above them to see the needs of a fellow human being. It is difficult for a person to act in selfless ways when she is focused on her egocentric needs or when she is filled with negative and harmful qualities.

Let's change the words we are using now from negative and harmful *qualities* to negative and harmful *energy*. Immediately, I envision moving from something that we associate with "hard and fast" (e.g. "The mineral he held in his hand had an iron-like quality") to something that is moving (e.g. "He was brimming over with the energy of enthusiasm").

Understanding Energy

This is the first thing we need to understand about energy. *Energy can move.* When we have experienced negative and harmful issues in our lives, they will always have been accompanied by negative emotion. *Negative emotion is a form of energy.* This energy remains in our body until we *consciously intend* to move it out.

We can do this by becoming aware that we possess it and by being willing to undergo a process of some sort to help us to discharge the energy. And until we do discharge the negative energy our bodies contain, it is very difficult to behave in ways that are considered to be divine. In fact it is very difficult to even understand what divinity is, much less be a fulcrum for its use.

And here is the conundrum. How can we possibly expect "the world" to behave divinely, when "the world" is fraught with the problems that serve to keep people disconnected from their inner wisdom and spiritually asleep?

The answer is simple. We can't! At least, not all at once.

All we can do is hope that one by one, people will begin to understand that a sense of divinity, a "heaven on earth," awaits them if they are willing to undergo a process of negative energy release by opening themselves to a new way of being. This is called healing!

More specifically, negative energy release is called *energy healing*, for it uses healing methods that people can learn to use to transform the negative energy they have within them into positive, life-giving energy. Once they acknowledge that they hold destructive energy (thoughts, memories, attitudes, etc.) inside and are thus able to label them clearly, release is possible.

Energies that leave them in constant inner pain and distress or cause them to despise themselves can be discharged. As long as people hold on to energies that cause them to despise themselves, they will be more apt to despise others who hold a similar energy signature or pattern.

Have you ever heard it being said, "I took an instant dislike to her. I don't know why"? The reason for this is simple. The first person holds a dysfunctional energy pattern that triggers a negative emotional reaction (feelings) in the second person.

How? The two energies attract, as energy patterns do, and the second person is confronted with an energy pattern within herself that is translated to her as *feelings* that make her very uncomfortable.

Why? It does not mean that the first person's behaviour resembles that of the second. But it does suggest that the first person's energy contains a pattern that triggers an emotional reaction in the second because *she holds a similar dysfunctional energy pattern within herself.*

So what? If this happens to you, it always suggests that there is something you need to acknowledge within yourself that is being reflected to you through the immediate feelings you experience when you are around this person. This dysfunctional energy is preventing you from experiencing divinity within your own being or from seeing the divinity within the other person. You may need to do some journalling around your reactions to see if you can determine its origin. To do this, you need to "write into your feelings" and fully describe what you *feel*, and in your description, see where this leads you.

It is quite possible that the energy pattern has developed as a result of some form of emotional pain, or perhaps abuse, that you have experienced in the past. Once you have been able to acknowledge this dysfunctional energy you hold, you may then bring your healing intention to it and begin to release it. (You will read about intention as a way of healing in Chapter Five.)

Your gauge to knowing if and when you have released it fully is the presence or absence of energy the individual reflects to you in the future, which will continue to be experienced through your feelings. When you have fully released the dysfunctional energy within yourself, you will no longer experience the feelings you had before when you were around this person! You will have been healed of this dysfunction.

The same type of interaction of energy signatures or patterns occurs with positive energy. Perhaps you've noticed that there have been some people you've just met with whom you have felt an immediate sense of compatibility. Afterwards, you may have even said, "He could be a friend, easily." And why? Again, you both possess similar energies. In this case, the interaction is positive and serves to connect you with the best part of yourself.

The energies have attracted on an unseen, inner energy level. And on an outer physical and emotional level, you react positively to this interaction. Not only does such a positive interaction feel very good, it holds a glimpse into your divine potential, for it contains positive, life-affirming, and loving qualities.

Human Divinity

To anyone reading this who has never before considered that anyone on earth—while still living—could ever be considered to have qualities that are divine, in the *formal* sense, you may be put off by what you are reading. But before you discard this book as being unworthy of your time, I invite you to think about this possibility in the terms I am offering for your examination and consideration.

I am suggesting that people are considered to have divine-like qualities when they behave in ways that project divine-like qualities—coming from the very best part of their human character. I am also posing two questions for your consideration: Why has man ascribed the word *divine* only to "the gods"? *Why,* when people react with complete and selfless caring and consideration of others, *can't their actions be considered divine?*

I have another "good-Samaritan" experience to tell you that happened to my husband and me while driving to Virginia recently. It happened following a coffee and bathroom break when we were heading back to Route 81 to continue on our journey from Ottawa.

We had just driven away from the coffee shop when we detected a noise that suggested the obvious—we had a flat tire. Already committed in the left of double left turning lanes, we were driving only thirty km/hour as we approached the traffic light and the turn, which would take us back to Route 81.

What appeared to be "luck" was most definitely with us because there was a service station on our right as we rounded the corner. "Luck" was again our friend because the transport truck that was beside us in the right lane slowed to allow us to pull over in front of him, that we might make our crippled turn into the service station.

Having gotten safely off the road, we got out of the car and went to remove from the trunk all of our suitcases and the gifts we had so carefully packed for this trip to attend our grandson's christening. With everything now out of the trunk on the grassy knoll beside the car, the spare tire finally exposed, we consulted the manual from the glove compartment. Although we had owned this vehicle for over five years, we'd never had to change a tire.

We had just reached the appointed page in the manual when a young man dressed in a white tee-shirt, jeans, and running shoes approached us, offering to change the tire for us! It was such a relief to have his help that it was only afterwards that we were able to look at the entirety of what had happened to see the divinity in all of it.

Some would say it was a series of coincidences; others would say it was synchronicity. Whereas I can understand both of these views, I am taking it a step further: I say it was nothing short of divine!

We were safely off the superhighway in a coffee shop before the tire began its deflation. It made itself known to us almost immediately when we pulled away from the coffee shop and were driving slowly. There was a safe place immediately available for us to get off the highway to change the tire, and we were able to move off the highway safely to drive into the service station. And finally, we were given a set of young hands to do the work.

When my husband offered to pay the young man for his kind service to us, he refused. To him, it was simply a need he saw, to which he responded. He and his wife were also travelling (home) to Virginia, still several hours away. He could have ignored us. We wouldn't have noticed his ignoring us, since we were so entrenched in our own difficulties at the time.

I am well aware that many would disagree with me in suggesting that there was a *divine* energy present throughout the entire experience, keeping us safe and then sending us assistance to change the tire; and furthermore, that someone who lends a helping hand to someone in need is serving in a divine capacity.

This was an "ordinary, everyday occurrence," an experience that wouldn't make the headlines of any newspaper; but to us, it was *extraordinary*. The young man would never have considered it to be extraordinary, for he was only doing what seemed natural and normal to do. Divine experiences *can be* natural and normal—*are* natural and normal—for natural and normal people experience them and take part in them *all* the time!

Finding the extraordinary within the ordinary is part of what divinity is all about. In the example above, the divine nature of the young man's good deed would have been aborted had he accepted the payment my husband offered for the help he had given us. He would merely have represented "roadside assistance," taken his dues, and left—leaving us thankful for the help but untouched by the selflessness of his action.

Look around you in your own circumstances. When you try, you will find good deeds—the kind I am calling *divine*—happening *everywhere*, all the time. They are deeds that afford their "doers" an opportunity to respond to another with kindness and assistance without any expectation of reward.

But they *are* rewarded for this selfless behaviour through the wonderful inner feeling they experience for having given of themselves so willingly, particularly when their generosity of spirit is acknowledged and received with a gesture of gratitude—a handshake, a smile, or a heartfelt "thank you." The feeling that is generated is enough to make it all worthwhile.

In the preceding story, even the transport driver would have felt a momentary experience of this good feeling for yielding to us in our time of need. It is this kind of human behaviour that allows us to touch the potential of our own divinity.

We touch our own divinity by embracing our spirit, which is connected to the divine Source of all creation. It is because of this spiritual connection we all have with the Source that we quite naturally have the potential for divinity to be realized within us in the form or *presence* of our spirit. The opportunities to touch this feeling are available to us every day in the simplest of ways. We need to remain alert and allow ourselves to acknowledge them and to respond to them.

So you can see I am not speaking of divinity within humanity in terms that are difficult to understand or relate to. Everyone has had experiences like these, and most will have offered this kind of assistance to others, also. It is easy, however, to slip out of these kinds of divine-like behaviours and say, "The car behind me will probably stop to let her through" when you are in too much of a rush and traffic is backed up in your lane, making it virtually impossible for a car to turn onto the street.

It is simple acts of human kindness, such as yielding to another, that affect others in a positive way that can be called *divine*. And each person needs to be alert and aware to *receive* the potentially divine impact of those acts. To accept a driver's gesture to turn onto the street in front of him *without* gratitude is to miss the point—there is no divine exchange between the two drivers. In fact, divinity is withheld from the yielding driver, for his action is not being acknowledged. His action is not considered special or even mentionable. *Yet the potential exists in his gesture of kindness to touch another human spirit*—to touch divinity—within himself and the person who accepts his help.

All of this happens so quickly that it may seem meaningless, until you are forced to stop and read about it as you are doing in this chapter. I am highlighting this point because it is such an everyday experience, an ordinary experience that *can* be a *momentary, extraordinary experience* for both drivers, as in my example, and that can connect each one—momentarily— with the divine, positive part of himself. Or it can make him angry, frustrated, or impatient. Which interpretation would set *you* up for *your* day?

When we touch the divinity within ourselves—even though it is a momentary experience—the effect lasts long enough for us to feel good inside and to have a flush of positive energy wash through our system. It is enough to help us want to hold onto the feeling for a little longer. And when it happens at the beginning of our day, we just might be able to carry the feeling well into the evening.

My daughter tells a beautiful story of going through the drive-through at the Tim Horton's coffee shop early one morning in my community. As she was coming into the queue with her Virginia-plated Jeep, she yielded to a woman to go ahead of her in line. While she was waiting for her order, the gentleman behind her started up a friendly conversation from his car window, based on her out-of-country licence plates and the yellow ribbon on her bumper reading "Support Our Troops." When she approached the wicket to pay for her coffee, she was told that the woman ahead of her had already paid for it! My daughter very quickly picked up on this unexpected gesture of human kindness and reciprocated by paying for the gentleman behind her in line. Curiously, the woman on duty at the drive-through said that random acts of kindness such as this happen there quite regularly!

Simple gestures of generosity of the spirit portray the commonality we all share and leave us feeling wonderful inside. And with growing awareness of how this kind of good feeling has been shown to have a very positive effect on our immune system—and therefore on our health and well-being—we are encouraged to practise kindness more and more.

Another short anecdote illustrates this point. One recent hot, humid summer afternoon, I accompanied my daughter, her almost two-year-old son, and her ten-year-old sister-in-law who was visiting from New York City, to a small community in the Ottawa Valley known for its ice cream. After doing the tour of boutiques and antique shops, we went to its locally famous General Store for our ice cream treat.

It seemed only fitting afterwards to drive over to the river that runs through this village and cool off by wading in. The four of us were standing in the water, throwing flat stones across the waves to see who could make them skip the farthest. My grandson was, of course, unable to make his skip, but he could certainly throw them and happily watch them splash.

After we had been there for some time—our ice cream now only a pleasant memory—we noticed a tractor coming around the bend from the village. It was pulling a double wagon filled with huge round bales of hay— quite a sight for anyone to see, let alone a child growing up in New York City. My daughter and I instinctively waved to the farmer who, very naturally, waved back at us. No doubt, we were equally as interesting to look at from his vantage point!

Afterwards, as we were driving away from this lovely time spent at the river's edge, my daughter yielded to another car in the parking area. The driver waved his acknowledgement of this gesture, and my daughter waved back. Her sister-in-law then asked, "Why do you wave at people you don't know? We would never do that in New York!"

Respect

As we come to know this good feeling inside of ourselves and see how it can be generated by a simple exchange such as a wave to a stranger, we understand its special quality that we wish to preserve. One way of doing this is to respect the good feeling it creates and to not take it for granted.

And as we begin to respect the feeling, we also begin to respect where the feeling arises, for it arises from within. In all of the examples I have provided, it arises from an interaction with a fellow human being—and with a stranger.

Perhaps this tells us something about respect. As we interact through simple gestures of human kindness or generosity with people we don't even know, we are automatically respecting them, seeing only the best in them, and coming from the best in ourselves. Sometimes this same respect is not so forthcoming with those who are closest to us. And when it isn't, we aren't looking for the best in them, nor are we finding the best within ourselves. We are temporarily blinded from divinity.

We are all spiritual beings making our way through life. We all have the ability to be positively affected by the generosity of the human spiritual condition. And we all have the ability to be negatively affected by the withholding of generosity and respect—either that which we withhold from others, or they from us.

When we respect ourselves, we respect our entire aspect—body, mind, *and* spirit. And within spirit, we respect and honour the *divine* aspect of our spirit. The same goes for others. When we can begin to look at others—even complete strangers—with respect for the divinity that resides within them, we can begin to view *all* of humanity in a new way. And when there is respect for one's fellow man, everything changes. We rise above our way of viewing others whom we dislike. We learn to attribute the same potential for divinity within them that we are beginning to find within ourselves.

From this position, we find strength to improve our relationship with others, especially those who are close to us. Here we begin to build upon the common foundation we all share—a divine nature that is at our core, longing to be touched and embraced by *each* of us.

The world *could* change if we each took the time to go through the process of viewing our own selves with respect and allowing this concept to spill over into the way we view others. The trillions of dollars that would be saved on defence, policing, jails, and penitentiaries in North America alone— were we to view ourselves and others with respect—could be diverted to meet basic societal needs: the end of poverty, the provision of universal health care, and a full education for all those who wish to receive it.

Such proactive government programs would clearly impact and reinforce the self-respect of citizens caught within the clutches and complexities of misfortune; they would end the financial drain brought about by the development and utilization of reactive programming offering band-aid solutions.

I am enough of a realist to acknowledge that it would take centuries to bring about such a pragmatic change. But I am also enough of an idealist to suggest that a society filled with self-respecting and respectful citizens could change the world ... *would* change the world. But first, we need to respect ourselves.

To respect ourselves is to honour the divinity that resides within us, and when this happens, we see, respect, and honour the divinity that resides in others also. Thus, we come into a changed way of being: *we glimpse the potential of divinity throughout humanity.*

We *Can* Find Divinity Outside "The Church"!

The potential exists to find divinity throughout creation, for it is everywhere. It is even in our neighbour . . . in our mother-in-law . . . and the beggar on the street. And it is found in the simplest of real-life stories that happen to each of us.

"The Church" loses its usual definition as it loosens its hold over traditional boundaries and restrictions and liberates its members. In seeing the potential of divinity in *all that is*, "the Church" takes on a new meaning, no longer seen as an edifice of control, shrouded in mystery, by those who never enter. It moves outside its elaborate buildings to the street—not just to the jails, the soup kitchens, and the hovels that provide shelter to drug addicts, but also to the elite neighbourhoods, the office towers, and the government buildings.

"The Church" goes into these places not trying to convert people to a belief about divinity that exists outside of themselves, but instead to teach—through example—about *the saviour* they each have *inside* of themselves, enabling them to transform their way of being.

We minister to one another in office towers, government buildings, grocery stores, classrooms, etc., through our positive actions and our willingness to acknowledge one another's spiritual connection to divinity and the commonality we all share. We begin to serve one another in exciting, new ways, and through these divinely guided experiences, a better way of being is revealed.

Divinity is made manifest in the corner of our hearts through the simple touch of a healing hand, a sincere word of comfort, or a willingness to stop long enough to listen to someone who needs to share her inner pain.

We worship the Divine—in all that this means to us as individuals—in the beauty of holiness: in the sacred temples that are found throughout nature in our mountains, in our forests, by the oceans, in flowering meadows, by meandering streams and picturesque waterfalls; we are filled with the power of the *Holy Spirit*. The sacred texts of the Torah, the Kabbalah, the Bible, the Koran, the teachings of Buddha, the Bhagavad-Gita, the Brahma Sutras, and others, are preserved for the wisdom they hold, allowing their teachings to be found by those who wish to explore them.

"The Church" then becomes the place where daily life is lived and where divinity is no longer perceived as something that may never be experienced or possible within the confines of humanity. *And we become "the Church."*

And "the Church" becomes the world . . . the universe . . . where all are united in one principle: the divinity of man—*all* men and *all* women and *all* children, and *all that has life*. This is the view of the Church of the future: to see oneself, humanity, and all that has life in constant relationship with divinity—regardless of race, religion, ethnicity, or social class.

Inch by inch, the transition is made from seeing life as being fraught with problems to looking for the goodness that exists in all that has life. Learning to focus on this goodness brings more goodness into existence. As we live each day with a positive mental paradigm looking for the goodness in all that is, we begin to see the divinity that was there all along. We just didn't understand that it was there; or we didn't know how to find it.

Our eyes were blinded from it through historic societal and religious distortions that intercepted and confused the common view of reality. These are the barriers that separate us from seeing beyond the physical and going more deeply into our spiritual selves. As these barriers dissolve through spiritual teaching and understanding, our mental clarity is restored. We regain our spiritual sight. We see and understand a new way of being—*a new way of being* in *all* that we do.

One by one, the transition of seeing the divine in each of our own acquaintances is made possible. People are acknowledged for the divine creation they are. The spiritual equality of mankind is searched out and honoured, and gradually . . . ever so gradually . . . the world becomes a better place.

Deo gratias!

The whole earth is full of His glory.

Isaiah 6:3

THREE

AND HOW DO WE GET TO THIS PLACE?

The energy of the Divine waits for us to reunite with it.
Teachers such as Jesus, Moses, Krishna, Buddha, the Dalai Lama . . .
help us to find it.

How do we get to this place where we perceive the divinity that exists within ourselves and our neighbour, our family, our friends? How do we get to this place where we can perceive ourselves, humanity, and all that has life in constant relationship with divinity? Is it even possible?

A few months following the release of my first book, *energywellness.ca*, I had an e-mail message from my publisher saying that a gentleman had called seeking my telephone number. He wanted to speak to me about my book. I was away on holiday at the time, so it was several days before I was able to follow up on his call.

It turned out that he was an elderly gentleman who was most sincere in his effusive remarks about my book and how it had affected him. He explained how he had been a "God-fearing" man all his life, but just couldn't appreciate his religion. This book had opened a new perspective of life to which he could finally relate and endorse. But he left me with one intriguing question to ponder. He asked, "Do you really believe that you must forgive everyone . . . everything?" And then he added, "I don't want you to answer this now; I want you to think about it for a while."

After hanging up from this conversation, my immediate reaction was: *well, of course we must*. But I realized I was reacting in defence of what I had written about forgiveness in this earlier book. So I decided to do as he had suggested: to not provide an answer directly but rather to let the question sink into my being and wait and see what might surface.

At the next energy wellness workshop I was facilitating a few weeks later, I was sitting with some of the women during our lunch break and the subject of forgiveness was raised. One woman said how she had read somewhere that spiritual fulfillment is achievable only when you can forgive everyone and everything that happens in your life.

As she spoke further, I was reminded of the question that my book fan had posed. I listened attentively to the discussion that was taking place as a result of this woman's comment.

Eventually, I offered a remark for everyone's consideration. I said, "*I wonder if we eventually reach a place of energy detachment in our lives that prevents us from being adversely affected by things that happen to us that would previously have required our forgiveness?*"

In other words, I believe that it is *detachment* that allows for spiritual fulfillment. And, as I explained in this earlier book, detachment cannot be experienced without acceptance. And a certain amount of forgiveness is necessary to experience acceptance.

So the answer to my book fan's very poignant question, I believe, is to be found where these three very healing energies of forgiveness, acceptance and detachment converge. For it is here that it no longer becomes obvious as to which element is actually at play within any given situation.

The Healing Process

Let me give you an example to explain this in more understandable terms.

Let's assume that someone in your life who has been hurtful to you in your past and who continues to be hurtful to you has just directed another insult towards you. But because you have undergone a healing process of ridding yourself of negative energy around your issues with her, you have come to recognize that this is the way this person is—unfortunate as that may be—and that the only way to be with her is to fully accept this reality. And because of your acceptance, you have been able to forgive this person.

Acceptance allows healing to take place within yourself and in your relationship with this person. Acceptance is like a lens into her soul. It allows you to see that she is in a very negative place herself.

You are able to understand that her behaviour towards you is indicative of the negative energies she holds within herself—energies that she has been unable to release, perhaps even causing her to experience the *dark night of her soul*.

Once you have been able to fully acknowledge all of this and accept it, almost magically detachment occurs, i.e. *energy detachment*. The key that allows this to happen is acceptance. Without acceptance, you cannot detach.

But *with* acceptance, you can immediately move into the next stage of your emotional maturity and spiritual understanding. It is during this stage that you are releasing the negative energy from the hurt she has inflicted upon you that you have been holding within yourself. And with the full release of this negative energy, you are able to view this person differently.

You will now be able to have compassion for her. And through your compassion, you will be capable of offering your support to her—if you choose to do so—when she comes to you for it.

Now let's go back and explain energetically how you got to this stage.

On an energy level, because of your own healing, you have detached your energies from hers, for you will have released your own negative energies associated with your relationship to her. If she continues to behave badly towards you, you will not be affected or drawn in to her behaviour because you no longer possess any of the same kind of energy within yourself. It has been the common negative energy signature or pattern that you have both held within your being that has kept you in a negative relationship with her.

Forgiveness, acceptance, and detachment converge for you at the point when you release this negative energy from your being, or transform it into positive, life-affirming energy. And this comes about as a result of your awareness of a need to heal that which is in you that does not feel good, or which takes you into negative emotional reactions and behaviours in your daily life.

And as you begin to heal, you come into an awareness of the need to forgive the hurt you have experienced in your relationship with her. This requires a complete acknowledgement of the pain you have suffered and a willingness to release the energy of this pain from your being.

Gradually, as you come into an acceptance of her despite the reality of her behaviour, you are able to release more of the energy of the pain while beginning to be able to forgive her.

Eventually, with full acceptance, you are able to fully release the energy pattern that has held you in a negative and dysfunctional relationship with this person and you are able to detach completely.

Inner healing is complete when you no longer hold any of this destructive energy pattern within your being. It is also at this stage that complete forgiveness is possible and compassion follows. Any future bad behaviour directed towards you will not affect you in the same way. You will not be drawn into it, nor will you be hurt by it. There is no need to forgive what has not affected you. Because you accept the reality of the immature behaviour, and because of your newly developed compassion, you are able to forgive her in the very moment of her negative reaction towards you.

And it is this ability to *forgive in the moment* that further allows you to remain detached from the person's negative energy. It cannot break through or *attach* itself to you.

What follows is most intriguing. For with complete detachment of negative energy, *attachment* of positive loving energy is made possible. What this means is that an opening is created for a dynamic change in your relationship with this person. Any future relationship on your part will be initiated through the energy of love.

If she accepts your love, this love will help her to come into awareness of how her behaviour has affected others. She may choose to begin the process of healing the underlying cause of this negative energy-inducing behaviour. In the meantime, however, you will begin to relate to her in more positive ways because her positive energies and yours will attach or converge on a healthy level. You will exchange healthy communication and enjoy each other perhaps for the first time.

Experiencing love will help her to release the negative energy patterns that have held her in undesirable behaviours. Her energy and behavioural patterns will therefore change. She will be capable of becoming more loving.

Before moving on, let me just say that I am not condoning the acceptance of abusive behaviour in my remarks above. And I am not suggesting that anyone should ever have to go through a process of self-healing in order to live within an abusive situation. I hope it is obvious to readers that I am speaking of situations that can happen to anyone within one's own circle of friends and acquaintances. And above all, it is never the behaviour that is being accepted. It is the *person* who exhibits the behaviour we are attempting to accept. And sometimes it is because of *our* acceptance *of the person* that he or she is able to begin to change.

Now, let's return to my book fan's original question about forgiveness. In the process I have just outlined, the person who was able to "forgive in the moment" could not possibly have done this without having gone through a complete healing process himself—a process that demands complete forgiveness. And in so doing, he will have released the negative energy that resembled that of his oppressor.

This is an essential point to understand when we speak about energy. It is those negative energies similar in structure—attracting one another and attaching to one another—that create the need for detachment. In the healing and releasing process, negative energies of all kinds that have been held within the person's energy system throughout the body will have been released through various ways that I have outlined in detail in my earlier book.

For the benefit of those who have not read *energywellness.ca*, I will quote from a passage that quite succinctly summarizes the healing and release process:

> When we experience emotion—whether positive or
> negative—we experience the energy of the emotion. Positive
> emotion contributes to our harmonic resonance—the
> optimum flow of our spiritual energy. But negative emotion,
> or energy, creates a disruption of that flow; it slows it down
> and serves to separate us from our spiritual energy. As we
> experience more of the same kind of negative emotion or
> remember the event that created it, we reinforce the negative
> energy and it creates congestion in our energy system,
> making it more difficult for the positive energy to flow. The
> more congested we become, the more we become separated
> from the positive aspect of ourselves, and, in time, we may

consciously lose touch with the spiritual dimension of our being. Here, we live in an unbalanced state, becoming vulnerable to negative forces that surround us, since we have unconsciously aligned ourselves with negative energy.

As we begin the healing process, some of this negative energy begins to be retrieved from our memory and brought up to the surface for our examination. Here we talk about it, write about it, cry over it, and acknowledge it in all ways, and, provided we truly wish to rid ourselves of the painful aspect of this memory—the energy of the emotion—we mindfully (consciously) release this emotional energy from our being. This allows positive energy to flow once again and the healing process to take place.

Healing means that the negative energy is gradually released from our body's energy system, allowing positive energy to once again flow freely. As more and more of the negative energy releases, we become aware of other issues we have been holding onto—other negative energies brought up to the surface of our being for examination. As this negative energy is gradually released from our being, we become transformed as human beings to new levels of awareness. We become transformed through the effects of positive energy flow within our being. Consequently, we hold less and less of the negative emotional energy charge within our being that has held us captive to certain attitudes, beliefs, or behaviour patterns, for example.

As new incidents occur that once stimulated a negative response within us, we are able to react in new ways. We no longer react in our former negative ways. We may begin to do so, but we can stop ourselves within a thought or within a sentence and alter our accustomed reaction, because we are aware and conscious of our inner positive spiritual energy. Eventually, we react only in positive ways or with complete neutrality.

This is the alchemy of healing. It is the transformation of negative energy into positive energy and it can happen in an instant! It happens when we have been able to consciously release the negative energies of the past from our being such that we open ourselves to embrace the energy of our spirit, which yields new and positive reactions, attitudes and behaviours. It is in giving ourselves over—consciously—to our inner spiritual direction that we become transformed to a new way of being.

We no longer hold the negative emotional energy
within our being. The memory of events remains, but the
painful effects of the events have been healed. We come
into a new place of being that is one of acceptance of the
reality of the events, an ability to forgive and an energy
detachment from the effects of the events. This results in
our ability to render "detached compassion" to others who
share similar experiences. In other words, as we are healed,
we become a healing presence to others because of the
healing we have experienced ourselves.

Returning to our earlier example of the ability to detach from a friend's
negative energy assault, the above explanation of energy healing makes it
easier to understand how forgiveness can become something that happens "in
the moment," followed by compassion.

The answer to my book fan's question should also become obvious. We
must forgive everyone . . . everything . . . if we want to free ourselves of
harmful negative energy. The reason for this is found in the way we heal. We
cannot fully heal if there is any negative energy remaining within our
emotional wounds.

It is no different than having a physical wound that must be cleansed of
all bacteria and impurities to allow healing to take place. We need to release
all the energy of the emotional hurt and pain contained within our emotional
wounds to completely heal, emotionally.

Otherwise, we are just suppressing the memories of our heart-felt pain,
and the negative energy that accompanies the memories. As long as we hold
onto this energy, we are not allowing ourselves to be completely cleansed (and
healed) of this issue.

As well, we provide the perfect breeding ground for more negative
emotional energy to be foisted on us—like a secondary infection of a physical
wound.

Self-Respect

And I want to offer another way of looking at this also. To not complete the
forgiveness process is to not fully respect oneself! This may seem like a radical
statement. What does self-respect have to do with forgiveness? Isn't it the person
who has created our pain who should be on her knees begging with apology and
wanting to make amends? Isn't self-respect about waiting for this to happen?

What if this doesn't happen? What if this never happens? What then? At
some point, you need to realize that the way you feel inside is not going to
change until *you* do something about it. *It is only you who have the power to
do something about the way you feel and to change the way you feel.*

This is where self-respect comes in. It is you taking the initiative to change your way of being—to put an end to the suffering you experience as you wait for someone else to change (or not). *There is no personal power in waiting for someone else to change!* There is no self-respect in waiting for someone else to change—only disappointment and dysfunction.

It may seem like too much of an effort to forgive what you believe is so unfair. Or it may seem like too much of an effort to finish the process of forgiveness. Or it may seem too painful to have to deal with all the issues that arise as part of the energy healing aspect of the forgiveness process. It may be a lot simpler just to say "forget it," get on with life, and make the best of it all.

Many people do this and never reap the full benefit of completing the forgiveness process. *They never fully heal.* They go about living their lives while carrying a chronic and burdensome negative emotional energy charge deep within their being—like a physical wound that continues to fester. It affects everything they do. It keeps them from ever experiencing the fullness of their own spirit—their own divinity.

Were they to respect themselves, they would want only the best outcome for themselves, and not to be continually subjected to the chronic emotional suffering caused by the initial hurt they experienced.

Go Beyond the Physical with Your Mind!

To look at all of this from a position of human dignity and self-respect is to return to the subject of divinity—the divinity that we each have within us and the divinity that also resides in others. Perhaps if we were able to view ourselves from this perspective, it would be easier to forgive completely . . . everything. In being unable to view ourselves from this perspective, we remain unable to experience the divine aspect of life. We cut ourselves off from our spiritual potential.

But by considering the capacity for divinity that resides within each of us, we are able to see beyond the borders of ourselves as the physical bodies we have and appreciate ourselves as the spiritual dynamic we are—a spiritual dynamic with no boundary and in unification with *all that is*. From this place of being, we *can* forgive completely. We *can* support one another and love one another.

This is how we make the changes within ourselves that are fundamental to healing within the human race. They begin with a simple exchange between two brothers or two sisters, or a parent and a child, or a neighbour over the backyard fence.

If we arc unable to forgive our "brother," we will never be able to evolve to anything more than we currently arc. War will continue to rage between countries and between people—the war that is going on at some level inside of us (the microcosm) that so resembles the war on the outside (the macrocosm).

If we cannot love our "brother," we cannot love ourselves either, or *all that is*.

Getting to "this place" of appreciation for the dynamics of spirituality may be fraught with complexities or it can be filled with self-respectful anticipation and positive intent. The choice is yours. It's all in the way you perceive your life and how you *choose* to get to where you want to go—*if* you want to go—and *be* what you want to become.

Is it possible to get to this place? Is it possible to view ourselves and others from the perspective that we are each vessels for divinity?

This book is about how we *can* get to this place. If you can at least imagine yourself, humanity, and all that has life as being in constant relationship with divinity, you can begin to make this dream become a reality; you will be able to recognize divinity as it flows through the simplest of your daily activities. You will understand that *you are a vessel for divinity* and that divinity *can* be found *in all that is*.

I open myself to You this day as I surrender my whole self to Your guidance
and offer myself to be used in ways that will honour and respect You,
the Divine force that works through me
as I gift my abilities back to the universe
in service,
and in gratitude,
and with love in my heart.

FOUR

BLESSED ARE THE PEACEMAKERS

Blessed are the peacemakers, for they shall be called the children of God.

Matthew 5:9

During a recent women's wellness workshop, I was doing a breakdown of types of negative emotional energy that separate us from an inner sense of quiet and peace. The usual words were coming from this new group of eager women. I say "usual words" because everyone knows the negative emotional energies that separate us from a sense of inner quiet and peace.

Most have experienced these energies all too often. And what came out in this particular workshop was the comment that these energies can become *a way of being*. We were speaking about worry and anger at the time. And indeed, worry and anger are, for many, *a way of being*.

Since this chapter is dealing with peacemakers, it seems most appropriate that we examine both worry and anger closely and have an opportunity to really look at them as they pertain to us. How do worry and anger keep us from being peacemakers? We will begin with worry.

One Sunday morning, I overheard an elderly woman in my church say to the person next to her that she worries about everything. Imagine! She worries about *everything*. This really got my attention for two reasons. First, at her age, I thought she would have learned that worry is not a productive way of living. And second, and more important, since this comment arose from the pews, I was amazed that this woman had never learned to take her worries to *God* for resolution. Perhaps this woman's views are not as uncommon as I had thought. Truly, for her, worry had become *a way of being*.

Learn to End the Worry Cycle!

When I teach on the subject of worry, I draw a series of circles to suggest visually what is going on inside of us when we worry. We literally go around in circles over and over with the thoughts that accompany our worry. And always, we find ourselves back at the beginning filled with the fear that also accompanies this awful feeling of worry. And for those for whom worry has become a way of being, it seems that there is absolutely no way out of this mess.

Some people worry this way about a family member who doesn't arrive home at the precise moment he was expected. The worry circle starts and intensifies with each passing minute until the sound at the door signifies that the loved one is home. And then the worrying can stop.

The sound of the door is what allows the worrier to be temporarily freed of the worry circuit. She may even attribute the safe arrival of her beloved family member to the fact that she has been worrying. She has been doing this on his behalf!

This worrier is freed from her worry circuit until the next issue of concern presents itself. And then the same feeling of powerlessness overcomes her once again as she engages in this new and familiar cycle of fear-based worry.

So how does this woman make the transition from her present way of being to a new way of being where she can stop worrying about "everything"? First, she must become aware of the fact that for her, worry has become a way of life—and it need not be a way of life!

She needs to become aware of what worry is doing to her physiologically. It is not just a time of mental anguish. It has consequences that affect her physical body as well. The stress of worry creates physical tension in her body that could cause a temporary rise in blood pressure, for example.

When worry becomes a way of being, elevated blood pressure may also become a way of being! And as with most negative energies, the stress of worry temporarily suppresses the immune system. In fact, the effect of any negative emotion on the immune system has been proven to temporarily suppress its function. It is important, therefore, to become aware of what each worry issue is doing to your body!

Besides a possible rise of blood pressure and temporary suppression of the immune system, the stress and tension of worry can create shallow breathing, sweaty palms, and dryness of the mouth. The tension that builds within the body may also be responsible for muscle tightness, particularly across the shoulders, in the face and jaw, and in the lower back.

And worry can severely interrupt one's sleeping patterns, creating further problems within the body. If you are a worrier, think about how worry affects *your* body—now, as you are reading this. Are there any other physiological symptoms you experience when you are worrying?

Next, on an intellectual level, the worrier needs to really acknowledge all the worrying she does. She needs to actually list all the things she worries about. She needs to examine each one and see what is at the bottom of each worry. She can do this most successfully through journalling.

This may seem like an endless process to go through—journalling about each worry that you have; but if you are a worrier, I believe you will find it to be a most beneficial exercise. To journal about worry, you need to allow yourself to write about one specific experience of worry that you can easily remember. Select only one at a time. Write everything about this experience. Allow yourself to remember the emotion that surfaced during your experience of worry. Notice what locations in your body you felt the emotion. Label these clearly in your journalling. Write also about how your body felt physically. What symptoms do you remember experiencing? Recall and write about all the areas in your body where you remember feeling tension and stress.

Then switch your attention to your spiritual self and try to remember how you felt spiritually while you were worrying. For example, did you feel connected to yourself spiritually? Did you feel the way you do following a meditation experience?

Do not attempt to mix all your worries into one subject for journalling. To do so is to enter into a pseudo-psychoanalysis of *why* you worry, and this will defeat the purpose. The journalling exercise is about getting in touch with each of your emotions that are at the base of your worries.

When you journal each worry separately, you are allowing yourself to become more intimately identified with all of your emotions, and in the process, you will learn something about yourself that will help you make the transition out of worry as a way of being.

Then, really begin to dissect each worry subject. Ask yourself the following question: Is it reasonable to be concerned? (Yes or no.) If you answered "yes," then take action. *Do something* about the worry you are holding. If you need to make a phone call to inquire about something or someone, do it. Or if you have to speak to someone face to face about the source of your worry, then do that.

Do whatever you need to do if it is appropriate to be concerned. And understand when it is inappropriate to worry. Could your worry be a camouflaged form of control, or an inability to let go of control over something or someone in your life? Or is it possible that it is simply a habit?

If you answered "no" to the initial question—*Is it reasonable to be concerned about this?*—then stop worrying. At least *try* to stop worrying. In fact, stop using the word "worry" to describe and think about what it is you are doing.

Next, as part of the spiritual exercise of making this transition, you need to be able to look to something outside of yourself to help you to remove worry from your life. For those who hold a belief in a higher power, this is the time to pray and to trust in a positive outcome.

For example, the parent who always worries until everyone has returned home can say a prayer for the safety of the person she would normally be worrying about and for his safe return. And then she needs to allow herself to trust. *Let go and let God!* The anxious parent's ability to do this will release her from the habitual worry circuit that has entrapped her throughout much of her life.

When you are in the process of making the transition from worry as a way of being, you will need to remind yourself every few moments, perhaps, to trust. Trust is something that needs to be cultivated. It cannot just magically unfold as a tool to use because one day you decide to use it. So in the early stages, you may find that you are still falling back into the worry cycle.

The key here is to acknowledge this intellectually and then find the pathway out of the worry cycle through prayer, perhaps, or through a positive intention to stop worrying and then through learning to trust.

The positive intention to stop worrying is, in itself, a de-stressor. It creates a positive mental shift within the worrier, which allows you to "let go" of the worry and to engage in trust. If you do not hold a belief in a higher power, you may go straight to trust. In trust, you are acknowledging that you have no control over the other person's destiny. At the same time, you are trusting in the best outcome for him.

Let's return again to the example of the woman who is worrying about her family member who is late arriving home. If the family member is one of her adult children, the only control she has is now in the past. Hopefully, she imparted teachings of safety to her child when he was young so that he is able to make choices on his own that are going to serve him well.

And, as a parent, she will have been responsible for ensuring that his safety and well-being have been addressed and fully understood by him in all new areas of discovery and activity as he was growing up. Beyond this, his life must now take its own course. She has fulfilled her role as parent and guardian. She cannot continue to be with him to ensure his safety. She must learn to trust that he can do this for himself. And much of learning to trust is letting go of "control over" others.

Trust, regardless of whether one believes in a higher power, is quite achievable if these teachings have been a part of your child's life as he is growing up. Children must be given graduated opportunities to become responsible so that they become independently capable of looking after themselves by the time they reach adulthood. When you have done this for your child, there is no need to worry that he cannot look after himself, nor to continually "check in" with him to ensure his safety and well-being. It is these behaviours by a parent that thwart an adult child's ability to become responsible, secure, and self-reliant.

So part of the pathway out of the worry circle is common sense. Does the person have the capability of finding his way home safely or not? If he does, then it is senseless to worry. If he doesn't, then worry is an inappropriate response to the situation. Action is required to determine why the person has not returned home!

Worry is only meaningful as it highlights an imbalance at the level of one's spiritual life. When anyone spends time in worry, this is a reflection of a suppressed spirit that has become overshadowed by the mental activity of worry. This imbalance actually prevents a sense of spiritual empowerment from unfolding in his or her life.

Worry is one emotion that must be understood as the balanced-living inhibitor it is. It needs to be eliminated by anyone wishing to engage in a journey with her spirit. And, as already stated, worry may also represent a lifelong, habitual way of being or of attempting to retain control over someone else's well-being.

If, as parents, we spend a lot of time in worry, we pass this useless habit on to our children. For, when worry is a way of being, it most certainly has become a habit—and our children learn many of our habits. So not only do *our* continuous worry patterns create an imbalance in our lives mentally, emotionally, physically and spiritually, we pass this dysfunctional way of living on to our children as well!

Just for Today, Do Not Anger[5]

Now, let's take a look at anger. Anger may also have become *a way of being* for some, especially if they have grown up in a household where anger was experienced daily. They will have learned to react with anger inappropriately to simple, everyday issues and activities. For them, anger will also have become a habit! Much relearning is required to bring about change in people who have experienced anger in this way.

If this has been your experience with anger and you wish to disengage from anger habitually, there are some fundamental things that you can do. First, as with worry, you need to dissect your own anger by looking at the kinds of things that arouse anger within you. It's best to write these things down so you can keep track of each one as you move into a series of questions about your anger.

Now you are ready to ask yourself the following simple questions with each situation you have identified in which you react with anger:

- Is it appropriate to get angry at this?
- Does it make sense?
- What purpose does anger serve in this situation?
- Could there be a better way of reacting?
- How would *I* feel if someone were to get angry with me in this situation?

And then consider this final general question:

- How does it make *me* feel when someone else expresses anger with me or around me?

If you cannot be objective in your consideration about the way you react with anger, you will not be objective about the way you will answer these

---

5 Spiritual precept taught in the practice of Reiki.

questions, either. If this is your situation, then you need to take these questions about yourself to a trusted friend or life partner, preferably someone who does not react in anger himself or herself at most things.

If you have no one you can do this with, then it is advisable to take the subject to a professional counsellor who can help you to work through these questions in order to make some profound life changes.

Anger can be a very positive emotion in certain instances. For without the emotion of anger, many very positive societal changes would never have taken place throughout history. But this is not the kind of anger I am speaking about in this chapter.

As recently as one generation ago, it was considered normal to spank a child, in anger, when one had become desperate in attempting to get the child "to behave." Today, parents who spank their children will suffer many consequences of this behaviour. Times change. Societal expectation of what is considered "normal" behaviour changes.

I recall how certain teachers of mine in the high school I attended used anger and threats and the occasional throwing of chalk or a blackboard eraser to keep students under control within the classroom. Sharpened pencils were poked into one's ribs for slouching or inattentiveness—startling, to say the least! Attending these classes was very stressful, as can only be imagined. And in the elementary school I attended, the threat of "getting the strap" if we were to step out of line was a constant concern on the horizon of all our minds.

For children, this threat created at least two messages. First, it was okay to use this form of discipline with a child. And second, it was not safe to step out of line—whatever that meant. In hindsight, it could only be perceived as a constant inability to fully express oneself at school or at home, for similar methods of discipline were used in the home as well. Today, any teacher using these forms of teaching behaviours would lose his or her job.

Thankfully, today's civilized societies do not accept inappropriate anger as a reaction to a situation that simply does not deserve anger. Anger management courses have become quite popular over the past couple of decades to help people learn to release anger from their lives and to redirect their energies into something less volatile and more productive. Child abuse is taken very seriously by society, with stiff penalties for parents, including immediate removal of children from their care.

This represents significant evolution towards the development of a peaceful society. Still, parents need to be careful not to abuse their children with words—the stuff of wounds that can run even deeper than those caused by a physical strapping.

If you were exposed to anger as you were growing up as a matter of daily routine, and if you felt threatened by it, chances are you have a lot of issues that are anger-based or anger-related. Some of these issues may be serious enough to require some professional counselling and subsequent complete acknowledgement to allow you to move through them so that you can make important life changes. If this is *your* situation, you are well advised to seek out the appropriate help you need.

The exposure to anger or the threat of anger on a daily basis—as a routine reaction to the simplest of incidents—creates an underlying fear in an individual. It may also create a need to *prevent* an outburst of anger in a parent or family member by trying to act perfectly. Children will cope with anger however they can, up to and including seeing an outburst of anger directed towards them as meeting a dire inner need to receive much-needed attention.

Anger within a household can lead to any number of dysfunctional behaviours in developing children. For this reason, as an adult there is a need to take stock of your own emotional inventory as it relates to anger.

How do you perceive anger? Do you consider it as a normal or healthy outlet for pent-up emotion? How often do you react with anger in your day-to-day life? Are you uncomfortable with anger? Are you uncomfortable being in a room when someone reacts angrily? Do you withdraw, either physically or emotionally, when anger presents itself? Do you react to someone else's anger with anger of your own? Do you react with anger at the slightest provocation? Have you ever experienced rage within yourself, or been the victim of someone else's rage?

When I speak to students or personal clients about emotions as having an energy component, one of the easiest concepts they are able to grasp is this idea about anger. Most people have witnessed someone who is angry. They have seen the redness in the face; they have heard the increased volume of the voice; they have either observed or been on the receiving end physically or emotionally of the violent behaviour and actions expressed by an angry person. Anger can impact us quite harmfully, even when the anger has not been directed towards us. *Simply being a witness to anger creates an emotional reaction within the observer.*

It is not difficult to imagine anger as being comprised of energy that has a unique and powerful force behind it. Dysfunctional anger contains an extremely negative and destructive energy. Its impact on those who are exposed to it, therefore, can be extremely harmful.

But the good news is that because anger as an emotion is *energy*, an individual who reacts with anger (or who has been negatively affected during his life through the accumulation of this harmful energy) can learn to move this negative energy out of his system. And indeed, it must be moved out of one's system—or transformed—for healing to take place.

As with all energy healing, the first thing that an individual needs to do is to become consciously aware of the impact that anger has had and continues to have on his or her life. And then, if anger has been the cause of emotional or physical abuse, or continues to be the cause of abuse, professional assistance may be needed to help the person to fully acknowledge this reality as a starting point in continuing the healing process. I say "*continuing* the healing process" because awareness followed by acknowledgement are the starting points of any healing process.

Journalling, a Healing Tool

As with worry, journalling will be a helpful tool to identify, acknowledge, and begin to release the energy of anger. This time, however, the process will take on an additional dimension of healing. So we need to look at the journalling process again.

As you did with worry, begin by writing about the effects of your exposure to someone else's anger, incident by incident. And in your writing, you need to record each incident as you remember experiencing it. Try to get in touch with and face your memory of the feelings you experienced at the time of the incident. This could become quite a painful process, and you might want to have a supportive family member or friend whom you can be with afterwards to comfort you.

The memory of the way that the incident affected you back in the past may cause you to become angry yourself. You may need to shout or scream or punch a pillow, for example, to allow the energy you have within you to escape. And you may need to cry and cry and cry.

Remember, you will have energy inside of you that has been bottled up for many years and if you are serious about your own energy healing, you will want to give it an opportunity to leave your body. So allow your body to go through this natural way of releasing the energy that has bound it up over the years.

And then, you need to comfort this part of your self that suffered many years ago. To do this, you may imagine yourself—during the incident of your memory—being comforted by your current self. Spend enough time on this phase of the exercise to truly allow your memory of yourself to be completely comforted with tenderness and sensitivity, with stroking, hugging, and healing words. Reassure this part of yourself that everything is going to be okay, as though you were a parent comforting your child.

After you have completed this part of the journalling exercise, shift your focus to how you feel *now* as you recall this incident. Is there any change in your emotional or physical state now, as you reflect back upon the earlier incident of anger? Can you link your present thoughts about the experience with the emotion you experienced in the past?

According to Louise DeSalvo, it is this ability to link feelings with events and to assimilate the meaning of an event into one's life that diffuses its power. In her book, *Writing as a Way of Healing*,[6] she reports on important clinical research conducted by James W. Pennebaker[7] and his associate Sandra Beall. Pennebaker and Beall were able to show that writing that describes traumatic events and our deepest thoughts and feelings about them, past and present, is

---

[6] Louise DeSalvo, *Writing as a Way of Healing, How Telling Our Stories Transforms Our Lives* (Boston: Beacon Press, 1999), p. 22.

[7] James W. Pennebaker, *Opening Up: The Healing Power of Confiding in Others* (New York: Morrow, 1990).

linked to improved immune function, improved emotional and physical health, and [positive] behavioural changes.[8]

Writing is, therefore, an important tool to help to release anger as a way of being in one's life. It helps to diffuse the power of the negative energies that arise as we undergo various thought processes. Pennebaker's research involved writing for only short periods of fifteen minutes over a four-day period. So the exercise does not need to be lengthy to be effective.

But if you wish, you may take the exercise deeper and write everything that is inside of you to be written about, purging yourself of what needs to come out and be acknowledged by your current self. If you decide to do this, be brutally honest. No one needs to read what you are writing. After you have done the comparative exercise of *then and now*, see if the exercise wants to take you anywhere else.

As you journal in this manner, you begin to touch your spirit and soul, and the process flows into a spiritual one; it is no longer just a mental exercise. Our negative emotions are like messages from our spirit. (I will be speaking more about this in a later chapter.) By writing into an emotion, you are actually writing into your spirit. Here, your spirit will interpret the meaning of the emotion's message, and by mentally acknowledging this information, you will be able to eliminate this emotion's harmful root from your body and mind. Journalling is, for many, an effective healing and transition tool.

Some journallers like to destroy what they have written by tossing their pages into a fireplace and watching them burn, seeing this as part of an empowering release from the things they have carefully recorded. Alternatively, the pages may be shredded and the tiny pieces seen as many parts of a former issue that is no longer complete and therefore no longer a threat.

When you have finished writing, you need to take a break from the intensity of your journalling. This is a good time to engage in something physical, like getting outside for a fast-paced walk. Often, more thoughts will arise as you are walking, because what you have begun in your journalling is a dialogue with your spirit.

And once begun, your spirit will continue to prompt you with insights and related answers that you are searching for. The receipt of insight is part of the healing process, for it provides you with information you need to be comforted within the process and to help you to let go of the destructive energies you have been holding.

I must enter a word of caution here: the journalling process can create a difficult period for you as you are put in touch with bad memories over again—memories you would prefer to forget. So always be mindful of the potential need to receive short-term counselling on the subjects you are

---

8 Louise DeSalvo, *Writing as a Way of Healing*, p. 25.

raising, if the experience is too painful for you to go through alone. This way, you will receive the professional help you require to allow you to continue in the process of releasing all that needs to come out.

Energy Healing

As well, it is at times like this that energy healing methods are particularly useful in both helping to continue the process of inner healing and in providing spiritual connection and comfort to the body and mind. I am speaking especially about Reiki, because of the gentle nature of its hands-on quality—very soothing for one who is in emotional pain.

Other forms of energy healing may be helpful also when attempting to release all of the negative energy from your system associated with anger. One of these is breath work. Students are supervised through a specific type of breathing that stimulates images, memories, and feelings.

By getting in touch with these images, memories, and feelings, the student is then coached to be with all of this long enough to fully acknowledge it and then to use the breath to help to release this energy from the system. This can be very intense and painful work and requires supervision throughout. It should not be undertaken by anyone until he or she feels truly ready to go through the process.

In fact, the body, quite spontaneously, can take a person through breath release work when it is ready to do so, and an individual may wonder what is happening to her as she continually feels the need to exhale forcibly. But eventually this need passes and so, too, does the energy that caused it.

Massage is a form of energy healing that will assist in releasing long-held tension in the muscles arising from the effects of anger. In many situations, the way a person holds his body is the result of underlying tension that has built up over his lifetime. Some of this tension will be caused by day-to-day stress, and some of the tension will be directly linked to the way he has reacted to personally related stressful events.

In all likelihood, he will be unaware that he holds this tension within his body. It has become a part of who he is, but a therapist will be able to feel his tightness and will most likely comment on it if he comes for massage therapy.

Although not always, it sometimes requires an aware and conscious mind—intent upon allowing the emotional energy held within this muscular tension to surface—for the energy release to be fully effective. Otherwise, the massage is something that just feels good, and its full benefit may not be realized. Approaching massage with *intention* for releasing emotional energy will amplify the results.

Other forms of energy healing that deserve mention here—also in terms of their therapeutic value in assisting with release—are Polarity Therapy, Yoga, Thought Field Therapy, Tai Chi, Chi Gong, Shiatsu, Therapeutic Touch, and, of course, affirmations and prayer.

To truly leave anger behind and unable to penetrate your life any longer, it is very helpful to have a role model who does not react in anger habitually. When you observe someone else's peaceful reactions to incidents that arise that would normally cause you to react with anger, you will begin to learn new and positive ways of reacting yourself.

You will begin to see how anger has been an inappropriate vehicle in your life through which you may have unknowingly engaged in other inappropriate reactions and behaviours.

And how does one feel when the energy associated with anger that has resided within his system for much of his life has successfully been released? Can you imagine how he might feel? Think about this for a moment yourself. Since the opposite of anger could obviously be considered peace, then perhaps it is a feeling of peace that replaces the energy of anger.

Indeed, this is the case. Initially, the feeling of release is a feeling of space within one's being. And then the space is filled with a new sensation that washes over one's entire being—a peaceful feeling of relief. And herein, the individual is able to rest and eventually celebrate a new way of being. Healing of anger thus helps to create peace within the soul.

Other soul peace-inhibitors are guilt, resentment, jealousy, regret, low self-esteem, fear, and insecurity, to name only a few. With any of these emotional states residing within one's being, it is difficult to maintain a feeling of peace for long, and thus care needs to be taken to transform the energies associated with these emotions as well.

"Blessed are the peacemakers, for they shall be called the children of God."

This Beatitude suggests that a life of peace is a life that is childlike. And certainly, in the early stages of release from destructive emotion, when the feelings of inner peace are experienced in the body and mind, the individual is returned to an almost blissful, childlike state, no longer victimized by the assaults that have formerly taken place in her body and mind.

This childlike feeling of peace allows a person to touch and to feel a sense of closeness to her own divinity, gratefully acknowledging that which has let her recover this part of herself once again. And in the throes of these intense feelings, the individual is committed to holding on to this new way of being.

Once healed of the effects of anger, an individual is now able to use compassion as part of her new way of being. And through compassion, she naturally spreads peace in her interchanges with others. Such benevolent compassion has the effect of also allowing others to find the place inside themselves where peace resides.

The more compassion we can exercise in the world with one another, the more peaceful the world will be. Think about it. We *each* have the ability to do this as individuals. We each have the ability to be peacemakers within our own family units and circle of friends.

We must first admit, identify, and acknowledge the *lack of peace* that we have in our own being and commit to a process of releasing *all* that takes us out of a natural and peaceful state. We will then find the precious child that still remains intact within us all at the level of our innermost spiritual selves . . . our own divinity . . . and *we* shall be called *children of God.*

In the circle of life, we all come from Divine love.
Our objective, on earth, is to learn to live in Divine love
before returning again to Divine love.

FIVE

INTENTION AS A WAY OF HEALING

There are many ways of engaging one's spirituality.
Healing intention is one of those ways.

Much has been written about this most powerful form of working with energy. The expression, "Be careful what you ask for, for you might just get it," is an example of the powerful aspect of intention. When we set our minds to do something, we are *intending* it to happen. This determination seems to take on a force of its own—an energy—that drives the outcome to meet our desired result. This energy can work *for* us or *against* us, which is why the expression above is actually one of caution.

Intention is a two-edged sword. Therefore, if we habitually make negative statements about our health, such as, "I am always tired," we almost surely will always be tired. If, on the other hand, the always-tired person says, "I am less tired than I was yesterday," her energy will respond accordingly—provided there is no medical basis for her continuous fatigue. Such is the "power" of intention.

Affirmations

Affirmations are good examples of utilizing this power of intention in our own healing. We may make a statement of affirmation that is quite specific, such as: "I am healing my cold sores." To reach the desired outcome of this affirmation, we may find ourselves embarking on a journey that leads us in a different direction—for the source of this viral eruption is quite likely stress. The affirmation, therefore, will lead us on a journey of learning to deal with stress.

As part of this journey, we will learn to identify what causes our stress and we will hopefully learn to find new ways of managing our stressors. If we don't, the cold sores will persist. As we work with the simple clarity of the original affirmation, our spirit will guide us through the maze we have entered—the maze we have created through our own reactions to stressors—to resolve our issues of stress, and subsequently encourage the cold sore virus to become dormant.

Once engaged, healing intention ceases to be mindfully directed. The original affirmation, "I am healing my cold sores," is indeed a mindful direction. But once we have engaged our healing intention, we are also engaging our spirit and connecting with our spiritual Source. However, to derive the benefits that flow from this spiritual connection, we must remain aware.

Statements of healing intention are wonderful tools to heal and transform our lives. What seems like such a simple statement on the surface takes us to places that we could never quite reach if we were to set out mindfully to get there.

At the level of our soul and spirit, there is a much greater intelligence at play—an intelligence that knows what is at the bottom of the underlying problem that has been identified within the original statement of affirmation. Quite often, this information is not recognized at the level of our aware and conscious mind. If we remember that we are spiritual beings living within a physical existence, then it becomes easier to understand why this is so. *Our spirit is waiting for us to become aware of ourselves as spiritual beings.*

Conscious awareness of this other reality makes a major difference to our well-being. Healing intention allows the spirit to guide the body and mind through the healing process that it needs to undergo in the process of healing. It will guide us through the darkness we may have in our soul. It will help us to release the buildup of negative energy we have accumulated throughout our lifetime.

Healing intention requires that we be *mindfully ready* to heal that which our spirit will show us. It requires that we be aware, alert, and ready to respond and then be willing to let go of the negative energy.

To thus engage directly with our spirit, we need to acknowledge attitudes, behaviours, and ideas that we hold as *our own*, and then we need to be *mindfully* willing to release or change them. If not, the cold sore persists.

This is an important piece of information for anyone using this form of energy healing. Affirmations tap into our spirit through the use of healing intention. What starts out as a desire or intent to heal a cold sore can actually be a prescription for the reduction of stress-related behaviours that may also be at the bottom of high blood pressure and other stress-related disorders of the body.

Once engaged in the power of healing intention, we can stay with the voyage for as long as it takes to identify all the profound causes that might result in the nuisance spot on our lip.

There are many ways of engaging one's spirituality. Healing intention is one of those ways. Someone may never have experienced his own spirit in a way that he can express what his spirit means to him. He may have resisted any ideas of "getting in touch with his spirit," and quite possibly doesn't even believe he has one!

Yet, if he is open and willing to try the simple experiment of using an affirmation to help him with some aspect of his life, he will find subtly, but surely, that he experiences change. Then, if he chooses to add the ingredient of intention to his healing affirmation, he will begin to find himself engaging in his own spirituality—a powerful aspect of healing intention.

Using Healing Intention to Stop Smoking

Affirmations can be used to reverse many forms of undesirable behaviour. Let's take smoking as an example. If someone wants to stop smoking but lacks the willpower to do so, she may begin by using an affirmation such as, "I have the willpower to stop smoking."

This positive affirmation is a means of strengthening her mental belief that she does, indeed, have the willpower to stop smoking. It is a way of reorienting her mind to the need to stop smoking and her ability to stop smoking.

After using this affirmation for a week or two, she may switch to a more powerful affirmation of healing intention: "I am using my willpower to stop smoking." This affirmation takes her to a deeper level—that of intent—"I am." And thus engaged in intent, she begins her journey with her spirit.

As part of her journey—if she remains alert—her new awareness will allow her to see new opportunities coming her way that interfere with her smoking habit, or that highlight the need to be in a smoke-free environment. This is her "spirit at work" leading her into these opportunities. They are, for the most part, out of her control in the sense that she has not planned the opportunities. They just come naturally to her.

This is all part of healing intent. It is what happens when she connects with her spirit through her intent to make some form of change. But again, she must remain alert and realize that these "happenings" are arising as a result of her intention to stop smoking. Otherwise, she will miss seeing their relevance, or may even miss seeing them at all. Thus, the affirmation, "I am using my willpower to stop smoking," needs to be said frequently throughout each day to help her to maintain her awareness.

As she is led into situations wherein smoking is simply inappropriate, she will find that her desire to smoke has lessened to the point where she doesn't even notice that she has gone for several hours without a cigarette.

In time, she will be able to stop smoking completely and with little difficulty—that is, *if she chooses*; because even after her spirit has led her through avenues of opportunity to make change, she may actually *resist* making the change. And even *if* she chooses to change, something in her life may trigger the habit again; but by calling on the healing intention of stopping the habit, she can do so again.

As various negative issues are raised, new affirmations can be developed to help you rid yourself of the negative energy that accompanies each issue or memory. Always use the present tense and begin the affirmation with "I am releasing . . . from my being." And recognize that the affirmation process will, in itself, take you through potentially difficult emotional experiences that will help you to confront what you need to release.

So the smoker may engage in heavy smoking again until she understands the need to release whatever has been raised for her to see and release. With complete release, she will be more capable of ending her smoking habit completely.

As you work with affirmations over time, you will begin to recognize these experiences as part of your own healing process. Despite the discomfort that they may create within you, try to think of them as signposts along the way that are there to guide you through your journey and keep you on the right path. In time, with constant healing intention, the release will be complete and the discomfort will be gone.

Eventually, when our smoker has had a complete spiritual awakening, her body will simply reject the idea of having a cigarette. All of this can be accomplished through the use of healing intention.

Intention as a Spiritual Connector

Intention as a way of healing can coexist with one's religious beliefs, although it is not dependent upon such beliefs. The use of prayer helps to maintain the focus for healing and will augment the process of healing intention when it is used with sincerity and conviction. Other religious practices, such as reading inspirational passages from the Bible or the teachings of Buddha, for example, may serve to align one's healing intention within the familiarity of religious doctrine.

Yet, healing intention can take place completely outside a religious belief system. What is unique about healing intention is that it begins with a desire to take responsibility for one's health and well-being. In so doing, the individual wills himself to heal that which needs to be healed. *The strength to do this comes from within.* Connection with one's own spirit (which is connected to the Divine Source of creation and all that is) has already begun.

Intention can be a way of healing most things in our lives that develop as a result of spiritual distress, by virtue of its ability to lead us to the source of our problems by connecting with our spirit. Once this connection has taken place, we open ourselves as a vessel for the Divine to work within us to help us to look at our life and heal those causes of distress. We will be led through whatever personal challenges we must pursue in order to be at peace with ourselves and with those who form the framework of our lives.

If you are reading this and asking yourself whether you might try using the power of healing intention with something like an arthritic condition that seems to be worsening despite medical intervention, my response to you would be, it's worth a try! Start by using a simple affirmation such as "I am healing my arthritis." You may add the words, "with God's help" to make it even more meaningful for you.

By stating and restating these words many times each day, you, too, will be engaging your spirit to take you on a healing journey. Be prepared and ready, though, for change to eclipse your current horizons. Change will present itself to you in any number of ways. So remain alert, aware, and willing to see and embark upon what comes along.

Just as the person who wished to rid herself of cold sores was taken on a journey of identifying her stressors that gave rise to her cold sores, you also will be shown that which may have been hidden from your awareness before now. Becoming aware is the result of making a spiritual connection.

Without becoming aware, nothing will change, for you will not see (become aware of) what needs to be changed and the arthritic pain will remain the same or continue to worsen.

Your arthritic pain may not completely dissipate on your healing journey. In fact, the healing journey, being as it is a time of negative energy acknowledgement and release, may actually see the pain temporarily intensified as you work through your issues.

But if you can learn to react in altered or changed ways to the situations that normally place a great strain on you, your arthritis may be quieted. You can learn to release the negative energy (and its accompanying vibrational frequency) from your being such that you may reach a stage of experiencing a reduction in the severity of your symptoms.

The same can be said of any chronic condition that has a component of stress within it. All you need is a willingness to surrender yourself to the Divine for guidance so you may make necessary changes. With complete surrender, you automatically submit to a subsequent process of release of harmful negative energy that vibrates in disharmony with your body's natural state. As you release this vibration, you will be able to live a meaningful life and a transformed way of being—fully engaged in your own spirituality and respectful of the divine forces throughout humanity and the universe.

The physical aspect of chronic illness and pain can no longer have the same power over you when you journey with your spirit. Its root cause may even be identified during your healing process. All energy release, healing, and transformation that follow will leave you with a feeling of well-being— positive energy emanating from your spirit that fills your body and mind. And in this state, *anything is possible.*

All along the way, you will be gifted with *subtle energy changes that you can feel*, that reinforce the good work you are doing. You will become aware of the possibilities for further healing that exist within your being.

The negative energy that we store in our bodies usually is deeply embedded. In fact, it can take us into the "dark night of the soul" and hold us captive there for some time. This is such an important issue that I have devoted the next chapter solely to this subject. But with continued healing intention, you will eventually make your way out and you will see significant change in the way you view your life, and consequently in the way you feel.

Maintain the Connection: Continually Nourish Your Spirit!

It is essential to remain spiritually focused for these results to occur. For this to happen, you need to constantly nourish your spirit. So be sure to refresh yourself with rest and relaxation, regular exercise, nourishing food for your body and mind, and with the stimulation of those things your spirit loves.

You need to treat your spirit with the same respect you give your body and nourish it throughout the day, *every day*! Engage your talents. Get out into nature and enjoy the beauties and sounds available there in all seasons and at all times of the day. Listen to music that uplifts you. Immerse yourself in colours that you love. Respond to creative urges. And so on. All of these things nourish your spirit.

By nourishing one aspect of yourself, you are also nourishing other aspects of yourself. For example, as you ingest delicious and nourishing food as part of a well-balanced diet, it makes you *feel* good. It provides you with energy to be mentally alert and to take part in physical activity.

Taking a walk in nature makes you feel good; it stimulates your physical body and relaxes your mind. *It lets you connect with your spirit because the energy within nature is the same energy that is deep within you at the level of your spirit.*

These forms of physical, mental, and spiritual nourishment are essential when one is engaged in a healing journey. To omit any of these forms of nourishment is to block the healing process available to you. Your entire being—body, mind, and spirit—works together. When you are deprived of spiritual nourishment, you also experience a deprivation within your body and your mind.

When your body is deprived of exercise and sleep and a well-balanced diet, you experience physical and mental fatigue. Your ability to react with mental clarity is reduced. You then become vulnerable to negative emotion. Negative emotion then separates you from the positive energy flow of your spirit.

But when you accelerate the forms of physical, mental, and spiritual nourishment that you need, you will find that your healing process is also accelerated. And you will have the added benefit of inner strength and endurance to deal with the potentially difficult aspects of the healing process.

Developing Wholeness

The more you become aware of the necessity to nourish the *trinity of your being*—the body, mind, *and* spirit—the more easily will you be able to use intention to heal and transform your life and move into a place of *wholeness*, wherein your body, mind, and spirit can work (and play) in complete harmony.

In wholeness, you are able to come closer to the awareness and meaning of *all that is*. You will become aware of the impact that each of us has on one another, and on nature and the environment. Here, you will find gratitude for the abundance that is your life, whatever your own life story may be. You may not cure your arthritis, but you may reach a place within your healing process of being able to live with it more comfortably.

When you develop a healthy relationship with your body, mind, and spirit, you are less susceptible to falling prey to negative relationships with others. You are able to act responsibly and with care and consideration of others. You come into a peaceful way of being. You touch that childlike preciousness that resides within us all. And your new state of peace, in turn, will be ingested by *all that is.*

You will not only be doing something positive for yourself, you will also be gifting your positive results back to all of creation! For as you are healed, you become a healing presence for others. This is not a new responsibility to take on; it is a new way of being, which will be felt by all who come into your presence. All that you do will be impacted by this new way of being, for *you will have become transformed.*

And this is what healing is all about. It takes us back to our roots—to our most precious inner self where all knowledge of the universe is stored, where we understand that we are one with all of creation. This is where we effect lasting change, because all that we do is undertaken from a complete sense of wholeness—not only of ourselves, but rather a sense of wholeness in all that we do.

We develop the ability to see the complete picture in everything we do. It is this awareness that allows us to understand ourselves, others, and life situations in a compassionate way.

When our own container for divinity is full, we become an oasis for others to come to for much-needed rest and renewal from the stresses of life. And we experience rest and renewal for ourselves as well, through our continual connection with the Divine Source of creation . . . with *all that is.*

What we do not nourish within ourselves cannot exist in the world around us because we are its microcosm.[9]

Joan Chittister

---

[9] Joan Chittister, *Illuminated Life, Monastic Wisdom for Seekers of Light* (Maryknoll, New York: Orbis Books, 2000), p. 29.

SIX

THE DARK NIGHT OF THE SOUL

Hear my prayer, O God, incline Thine ear,
Thyself from my petition do not hide;
Take heed to me; hear how in prayer I mourn to Thee
Without Thee all is dark; I have no guide.

Felix Mendelssohn-Bartholdy 1809–47

These pleading words based on the 55th Psalm, "Hear My Prayer," set to chromatically beautiful music by the poet and composer Felix Mendelssohn, represent the essence of the dark night of the soul. The desperate petitioner is pleading to God for guidance and later imagines himself as having wings like a dove, that he might fly away into the wilderness and remain there forever at rest (from all his afflictions).

The healing and release process is, for many, a lengthy period of time. It is a time in which one may sometimes feel overwhelmed by it all—by its depth and the degree to which it can overtake one's life, often sending one plummeting emotionally into a downwards spiral.

The enemy alluded to by Mendelssohn's words that follow in this plaintive song of prayer is undoubtedly the enemy that resides within the petitioner—a feeling not unlike that experienced by anyone who is traversing the dark night of the soul.

The expression *the dark night of the soul* is sometimes used to best describe the intensity of this feeling and period of time of healing in one's life. In this chapter, I will endeavour to explain its meaning; although the more one looks into the dark night, the more one realizes that the dark night holds many secrets that reveal themselves little by little over time—or, perhaps, may never reveal their full meaning. Nonetheless, there are some aspects of the dark night that can be suggested here for consideration.

To begin, let me say that the dark night of the soul can be a complex time of potential confusion, creating a complete—albeit temporary or intermittent—masked suppression of the human spirit. And yet, it is also a time of immense personal growth, wherein the ways of the mind slowly learn to yield to the ways of the spirit.

The dark night can be triggered by the immersion into one's spirituality and the necessity and intention to heal the aspects of one's life that have served to separate him from his spiritual self. But this is not always the case. There are those who have discovered their spirituality following a lifetime of living the reality of issues that are not healed within their being. Having become immersed in a most beautiful expression of their human spirit, they experience only joy and thanksgiving at having found their spirit! Perhaps they also received the *miracle of healing* in having finally acknowledged their spirit!

For others, the dark night may be an expression of inner dissatisfaction of living a life that has been spiritually sterile. In becoming aware of something more, the dark night may intensify as the now spiritually aware individual strives to find his way back through the maze of what life has been to what life *can* be.

The dark night can be insidiously organic in nature, as it slowly makes its way into one's consciousness—its cause not easily tied to anything specific, and its recognition therefore difficult to pin down.

For some, the dark night will be experienced at a turning point in life—at a time when something within them has triggered a need to work through issues that have lain dormant, perhaps, or to face dysfunction that has determined the way they have lived their lives up to now.

Or the major trigger could be the extreme experience of loss, such as the loss of a job or a close family member—the lines between grief and the dark night blurred into obscurity, making progress through the episode challenging, at best.

The abyss can be experienced in many different ways, its intensity and the seriousness of potential complications varying within each individual. Regardless of how someone labels his or her own dark night, there are some areas of commonality, which will be experienced by most to a greater or lesser degree.

In all probability, it will be a time of reflection, of thinking back over your life and how you might have done things differently. It may even be a time of blaming persons in your life for the way you feel today. But blaming serves no purpose other than to hold you energetically in the same dark place until you can come into acceptance of these individuals through the process of forgiveness.

A certain amount of reflection serves to point out the precise misgivings you may be holding inside about your life, so that you may resolve them. It is important, however, to not allow yourself to get stuck in this stage. Getting stuck here becomes a most unhealthy way of being and could precipitate or extend the dark night.

For those who have begun to move through the negative energies they have been holding onto, the release process itself may lead them into the dark night.

For as we begin to release negative energy, we are forced to look at the issues we need to release—sometimes reliving them in our minds, over and over.

When this process becomes too painful, it is as though we are immersed in a dark night within our own healing process. It is almost like a rite of passage. We must be willing to give up the energies that have held us captive if we are ever to experience freedom and maturity from their hold over us. And freedom—spiritual freedom—is the reward for having traversed the dark night.

It is important, therefore, to have help at this stage to assist you to acknowledge your issues and to face them in such a way that you can willingly release their energetic hold on you. Positive affirmations and healing intention will help greatly with this process, reducing the length of time required to move this energy out of your system. And professional counselling may also be required. For those who hold a religious belief, this is the time you will look to your faith more than ever to help you to face each day and to somehow find the continued strength within your beliefs to find your way out of the darkness.

When issues are tragic and involve shame—such as sexual abuse—the dark night may involve a period of setting oneself apart from everything and everyone in one's life who previously played a large part. It can, therefore, be a time of rejection; and the individual may first of all experience rejection within oneself, and possibly even hatred.

When this feeling of self-loathing is severe or prolonged, the threat of physical or mental illness, including suicide, may occur. Professional help is *essential* for anyone who is suffering at this level.

On the less tragic side, it may simply be a time of confusion—of not knowing what is wrong, and not being able to pin anything down as the source of the confusion. Yet the darkness continues and reinforces itself amidst what is most likely spiritual distress.

Before going any further, let's try to summarize what has been suggested so far in an attempt to understand this probably all-too-common phenomenon. The dark night may occur:

- As a result of opening into our spiritual awareness and recognizing the need to heal the issues in our lives that have been hidden away within our being. It is our healing intention that *may* serve to take us into and out of our dark night as we work through all of the issues that need to be released—issues that temporarily separate us from the positive energy flow of our spirit.
- Insidiously as a result of spiritual distress when our spirit is attempting to get our attention to allow it to surface and take its rightful place in our life.
- As a side-effect of an experience of extreme loss, where we seem to completely lose touch with the spiritual part of ourselves amidst our own grieving process.

- As a result of the side-effects of abuse where the individual has a deep need for healing.
- As a time of immense personal growth, wherein the ways of the mind slowly learn to yield to the ways of the spirit. In this way, the dark night may be considered a rite of passage into the maturity of one's spirituality. "The purpose of the dark phase of any cycle," writes Demetra George, "is that of transition between the death of the old and the birth of the new."[10]

And as a last point, I think it is only fair to say that because each person is himself or herself an individual, there can be no precise definition of how the dark night will affect anyone, or even *if* it will affect everyone who fits within the "convenient" list I have posted above.

Spiritual Distress

It seems to me that the only thing about which we may be reasonably certain is that the dark night brings definition to a period in one's life when one is not in sufficient contact with spirit, such that spiritual distress—to some degree—is being experienced. And, I suppose, the greater the separation from one's spirit, the greater the degree of spiritual distress.

The words from Mendelssohn's prayer above actually provide the bottom line on the dark night of the soul: "Without Thee all is dark." This is the essence of spiritual distress—the inability to find the God-force *within* us. The God-force is the "sublime friend" we all have inside us, and which, according to the *Bhagavad-Gita*, we don't know how to find. And if we truly don't know how to find it, our days *will* be dark, for we will be continually searching for, or *deeply longing* for something and not knowing what it is that causes us to feel this way.

But there will always be those who do not suffer from spiritual distress and who will be completely unaware of the spiritual component of their lives, and we can only stand back and ask the question, "Why?"

Undoubtedly, positive mental attitude has played a large role for these individuals. Perhaps one person sees her life as brimming over with opportunities for discovery and adventure as she faces life's challenges in positive ways. The outcome of this positive mental attitude towards life suggests she is engaged in a positive energy flow of both mind and spirit—a very healthy combination. She is definitely in touch with her spirit even though she does not express her understanding of life in this way.

And for others, perhaps life is lived superficially with little thought given to the meaning of life, thus creating a subsequent lack of awareness of the spiritual dimension. If positive thinking and attitudes are not prevalent in this person's life, spiritual distress will most likely show up as physical illness—

---

[10] Demetra George, *The Mysteries of the Dark Moon* (San Francisco: Harper, 1992), p. 5.

the potential result of a life that is not engaged in the positive energy flow of one's spirit.

Spiritual distress is a symptom of the dark night of the soul. It is a symptom that means that the spirit is *unable* to express itself or that it is *attempting* to express itself. Either way, it cannot be fully experienced within its host body and mind and, consequently, it cannot be understood. It is stuck within and behind the areas of the mind that have kept it hidden—trapped— somewhere inside the physical and mental being in which it resides.

The mind is in control and is doing battle with the spirit to ensure that it remains hidden away. The spirit, on the other hand, is unable to fulfill its reason for being; it is stifled and unable to breathe its positive life-affirming energy into the body in which it lives. It survives only as an unidentified mystical persona and maintains this mystique, always seeking to fulfill its mission despite constant whipping back to its depths.

In the extreme, what flows from this secret place of residence by the spirit within the human body is any number of physical complaints . . . or quite possibly illness that affects the entire system, for it is a challenge for the immune system to defend itself against this invasion of apparent spiritless existence.

Or, the individual may suffer from clinical depression or experience a "nervous breakdown." Or, he might manage to cope from day to day amidst feelings of being lost within himself, finding solace in alcohol and prescription drugs, or addictive behaviours, dealing with a darkness that he cannot understand or explain and that becomes for him a "normal" way of being.

The soul registers what at first glance appears to be a spiritual problem, but it is not a problem within the spirit, per se. Actually, the body and mind are not acknowledging the spirit. The spirit is cut off by negativity of some form as a result of a buildup of negative emotional energy created through life's events. The soul, which records all of its host's life experiences, registers dismay. Let's look at this more closely.

The Duality of Spirit

The human spirit contains a duality of purpose and makeup. The first aspect of spiritual duality is the universal life force quality that it is—the same energy as that which is contained throughout nature. The human spirit therefore connects us to the *energy Source of all creation*, and in that sense is considered to be *divine energy*. It is completely positive energy, for it is the energy of divine love. It represents the innermost quality of the human entity in which it resides and is the connector to all elements of life, humanity, and nature; it merges, energetically, with all living things. The human spirit is timeless; it has quite literally been in existence since the beginning of time.

The soul, on the other hand, is the second aspect of one's spiritual duality—the part of the human dimension of spirit that bears the uniqueness of each person. It contains the entire lineage and history of one's being.

The soul is where our memories of timeless events are stored. It is what causes us to react emotionally to music and rhythms, words, and visual cues that we hear and see for the first time with an inner sense of knowing that they have always held very deep meaning for us.

It is from the soul that our emotions arise to be translated and interpreted by the mind and felt within the body as *feelings*. They let us know when our soul is disquieted as a result of a buildup of negative energy experiences in our life; conversely, they let us know when our soul is happy. In a sense, our emotions are like the voice of our soul, or messages from our spirit.

Our emotions of happiness and love allow us to align with the positive energy of our spirit—the universal life force—and to feel energized and renewed by its life-giving qualities. Emotions such as anger, guilt, and worry keep us from feeling aligned with the positive energy of our spirit. When we experience the dark night of the soul, we are predominantly experiencing negative emotional energy and the subsequent psychological and physical impact of negative energy.

It is as though the positive energy from our spirit is temporarily unavailable to us—disengaged by our immersion in negative energy.

Consider how you feel when your emotions are suffused with love. Do you feel both loving and loved? Do you have a light and healthy feeling within your body and mind—a feeling that you can do almost anything you want to do and that "the world" is a wonderful place?

Contrast these feelings with how you feel when you are frustrated by guilt or anger. The world is not such a happy place now, and this is partly because of the heaviness you probably feel in your body, possibly in your throat, chest, back, or upper abdomen.

What you are experiencing in these exercises is how positive emotion serves to connect you to your spirit, and how negative emotion seems to temporarily separate you from this wonderfully light feeling of positive spiritual energy, weighing you down energetically.

Try to imagine that the soul is like a valve that allows movement in one direction from your spiritual self into the rest of your being. The valve is always open to allow the positive energy to flow into you continually. And when you experience the energies of negative emotion, the valve prevents the negative energy from flowing back into and contaminating the positive energy of your spirit, for this is what valves do. They allow movement in only one direction.

This means that when you are embroiled in the negative energies associated with negative emotion, you still have the capability of receiving positive energy; in fact, the valve will still be open, allowing the movement of positive energy of your spirit and the universal life force to flow into you.

But somehow, when we are caught within the vortex of negative energies, we are not always able to mentally perceive the positive energy that actually coexists within our unique being. Because we are less able to perceive the positive energy, our minds remain focused on the negative energy.

As we focus on the negative energy, we effectively cut ourselves off from experiencing a positive energy flow throughout our being. Thus, the positive energy of our spirit is unable to penetrate our being while we are immersed in negative feelings, emotions, and behaviours. *Could these emotions we experience be our own unique version of a self-created Hell?*

Until, within the human dimension, we have learned to release these forms of energy and to detach from these energies, the valve remains functional, thus preserving the universal life-force in its purest form.

How About Creating a "Heaven-on-Earth" Reality Instead?

On the other hand, if humanity is connected to the universe through the soul, and thus the human spirit, the potential exists for humanity to create a life of positive, life-sustaining qualities that we can only imagine as being *Heaven-like*.

This is not apparent when we look around at the world and see the realities of poverty, crime, terrorism, and war, and generally, man's inhumanity towards man, making the world seem more like Hell than Heaven.

And yet, it is the soul of "man" that protects the universe from becoming contaminated by humanity's misuse of life energy. It is what I am calling a spiritual valve, allowing the flow of spiritual energy to move in one direction only, thus sustaining the purity of Heaven-like energies.

When humanity evolves to the point of asking the question, "What is life all about?" the answer lies in the underlying desire and spiritual need to find one's way back into this purest energy state wherein there is no contamination . . . only the purest, positive energy and life force. *Could this actually be the meaning of Heaven?*

Can we, therefore, create a "Heaven-on-earth" reality for ourselves if we can learn to live within the positive energies that are so aligned with our spiritual dimension? Can we succeed in releasing negative energies from our being such that we no longer attach to any of it? *Could this also be the meaning of Heaven?*

Can we ever perceive a life that is lived within the context of compassion and understanding, complete forgiveness, and love? Was this the meaning behind the symbolic teachings of Jesus? *Is this the Christ consciousness?*

Do we experience the *dark night of the soul* as we try to make our way back through all the misery of our human failures—not only of this lifetime but of those our mind does not even remember or comprehend—to glimpse the comfort and purity of the soul-remembered Christ consciousness where *all is one* and where the God-force of all creation resides?

Are our mental institutions filled with people who are trying to make their way back out of their own interpretation of Hell, but have lost their way? Is society filled with people who are frantically trying to make their way back but don't know how? Is the secret of the universe that we may choose to live our lives as though we are in Heaven *or* in Hell?

Are negative energies the result of a satanic force that is always available to us, tempting us into its brightness only to find instead a complete void akin to total emptiness—an abyss into which we fall when we are most vulnerable, and out of which we can only climb when we are given light to find our way?

And is this light the God-force that is always available to us, whose brilliance blinds us into incapacity, retreat or surrender? And in choosing surrender, do we find our way through the long, cold, and wearisome night into the healing warmth and compassion of the familiar light of day?

Life is filled with experiences that can create an inner struggle in the way we perceive them; but on the whole, we are meant to enjoy our lives. The positive energy of the universe is always available to us through our own spiritual self. It is always flowing into us. We need to understand that this is so and to acknowledge this positive energy gift with gratitude from moment to moment, day to day, and year to year.

Don't Give Up!

We need to find our way through the maze of obstacles to be able to do this. For some, it takes almost a lifetime to find their way through the dark night of the soul. For others, their dark night will be less severe or prolonged.

And sometimes, we hover around the edges of our own darkness, returning at the slightest provocation: an innocent remark made by a friend, a disrespectful glance from a stranger, a dark and gloomy day, the reliving of a memory of personal trauma or tragedy—even though we thought we had successfully made our way out through all of the darkness.

It is like standing beside the beautiful woods that are so familiar to you by daylight, yet were you to enter alone at night, they would seem to pose a threat of danger. And one certainly enters the darkness alone. No one else can possibly understand the exact nature of your personal darkness. Others may have experienced something similar, but no one shares your precise feelings. And there is loneliness in that.

And there may be depression in it—whether or not you need medication to allow you to cope with it—a type of mental paralysis that keeps you from reaching out to be pulled away from the edge of the woods and from the dangers that lie within.

The tendency is to retreat into one's own dark night when something happens to throw us off our spiritual path, and to return to the place that we know the best—the place we have gone in our minds, throughout much of our life—for protection amidst our own discomforts, our own spiritual distress.

There may be temptation to return to addictive practices or behaviours that are a struggle for us as we hover outside the edge of the woods, and a comfort to us when we are drawn back in.

This tendency is caused by the human frailty of our physical dimension. We retreat into our old habits and perspectives on life when things upset us, rather than erasing these outdated reactions from our being and confidently moving into positive new ways of viewing our life experiences.

When we are drawn back in through these habitual reactions, we need to make a concerted effort to resurrect ourselves from this place. We must do whatever will allow us to refresh ourselves within a positive energy flow once again—to free ourselves from the energy hold of captivity by the enemy within our mind.

This is the time to get outside into nature and go for a walk; eat nourishing comfort food; listen to inspiring music; connect with life-affirming friends; consciously stop thinking negative thoughts; pray for strength to come back into a positive framework once again; do whatever you normally enjoy doing to help you to align with a positive flow of spiritual energy and to disengage yourself—yet again—from the familiar and awful pull towards the dark night.

Spiritual Transformation

Perhaps the dark night of the soul is simply *any* experience we have that, for an extended period of time, takes us away from the feeling of positive energy flow such that it feels like a part of us is dying inside.

And here we remain until our own spiritual transformation can take place. Here we remain until we can be resurrected from our own tomb of despair, willing to accept the unseen hand that removes the boulder that has held us inside and now guides us back onto our path once again—stronger for the internal suffering and death we have experienced, and spiritually transformed because of the healing that has taken place within us.

For those who have been gifted with complete healing and spiritual transformation and the ability to live seeing themselves, humanity, and all that has life in constant relationship with divinity, there will be no more dark night.

The negative energy has been dispelled from their being. They have evolved to the point of finding Heaven in their daily lives and in so doing, they bring the meaning and possibility of Heaven's potential a little closer to those of us who are still evolving.

These are the spiritual beings living among us who are here to guide us through our own dark night—qualified to do so because of the experiences they have had themselves—now helping to illuminate the pathway for others, that we may find our way also.

And from this stage of evolution—spiritual transformation, and seeing oneself as being connected to all living things within the universe—most assuredly flows the understanding of the *divinity of man*.

It begins with a conscious awakening that takes us into and through the dark night and then into the light. Here, we may truly learn to live our lives from the potential and expansiveness of the human spirit wherein we may find divinity in *all* ways, always.

I remember, when in my late thirties, standing at the bedroom window of my beautiful home, looking out across the huge natural pond in our back property and into the woods that lay beyond, desperately thinking to myself: *Is this all there is?*

It seemed to me that all my investments of time and energy in my work and home life were not accruing any dividends. Despite the beauty and peace that lay before me—the giant ash trees that formed a perfect silhouette against the morning's crimson sky, and a country boundary against the distant glow of city lights at night—my life just wasn't making sense to me any more. There had to be something else, I thought, as I pleaded with nature to give me an answer—not unlike Mendelssohn's petitioner.

I had entered my own dark night and wasn't even aware of what that was. A lifetime of attending church each Sunday had not prepared me for what I was feeling now; nor was it to provide any answers in this time of spiritual distress.

And with no sense of having an inner spirit connected to *all that is*, I felt very alone and disconnected. Here I remained, barely coping inwardly at times, until I became spiritually aware—outside the church.

And as I have already pointed out, the side effect of becoming spiritually aware is to enter one's own healing journey. And within this journey, one becomes (re)acquainted with the dark night as he begins the spiritual transformation that must occur within his being if he wishes to pursue his own divinity.

Or perhaps I should say, he begins the spiritual transformation his *spirit demands of him*, so that he may realize the meaning of his own life and the evolving purpose for which he was created.

Conscious Surrender

The awareness of your spirituality while traversing the dark night allows you to find the directional signals throughout. It provides rest stops along the way, bringing you into the light for brief periods.

Here you receive the assurance that the light *is* there and the sense that the darkness—although difficult to manoeuvre—is slowly dissipating, creating a change in the way you are feeling, in general. It provides a very great sense of actually being guided throughout your own darkness, provided you are willing to *surrender* to its guidance.

Surrender is very much a mental transformation wherein you are learning to not be in control of organizing your life down to every last detail, as the mind is so capable of doing. Instead, the mind acquiesces to the spirit—over time. This results in an amazing change in the way you begin to live your life, allowing spiritual assignments and opportunities to come to you while remaining mentally alert to see them as "assignments and opportunities" and to mentally process their meaning as you engage in carrying them out.

And, having reached this stage of mental and spiritual transformation, the physical body is also in the process of transforming. It begins to relax in the presence of reduced mental and spiritual distress and improved positive energy flow within its being.

There may still be more darkness to get through before all the negative energy is released from the body and mind; but the understanding that *there is something else* lends enormous comfort. It concretizes one's spiritual search and makes it real.

In Summary

To summarize, then—having taken you through a spectrum of possibilities of what the dark night is, or *may* be—let me say this: The dark night of the soul is your spirit urgently telling you that it is time for you to pay attention to it and to let it come into your life and take its rightful place, to nourish you and comfort you amidst your life's many challenges.

And here is the secret to finding your way out of the darkness: *You must be willing to release all of the negative energy you hold in your being associated with everything you have perceived within your life to have been a problem for you.* You must be willing to perceive your life in new ways!

You need to be willing to soften into new attitudes of forgiveness and love and relinquish the hold of fear that has been your driving force. In doing this, your body and mind will be cleansed of their impurities. And finally, for your spirit to flow freely, your mind needs to relinquish all control over your life. *You must surrender to your spirit!*

And unlike Mendelssohn's dove, your spirit will not wish to remain forever at rest. Rather it will comfortably soar to the height of its possibilities within your life, thereafter sustained by the light. It is here that you will find inner rest from all that has created your dark night. Here, the morning light will not only be found within your spirit, it will be found in *all that is.*

And then, the morning light will lead you into a new way of being wherein you become aware of the necessity of your body, mind, and spirit to work harmoniously as one unit—each aspect respectful of the needs of the other—to achieve a sense of wholeness, from which purposeful living is possible.

If you are someone who is experiencing darkness within your own soul, try to take some comfort from this information. There *is* something else! Your spirit desperately wants you to know this.

And if you will just acknowledge and trust your spirit and then surrender to its earnest promptings, it will guide you safely through your own darkness and out into the comfort and assurance of the light once again.

Come to Me, all who are weary and heavy-laden, and I will give you rest.
Take My yoke upon you and learn from Me, for I am gentle and humble in
heart, and you will find rest for your souls.
For My yoke is easy and My burden is light.

Matthew 11:28-30

SEVEN

WELCOME, HAPPY MORNING!

"Welcome, happy morning," age to age shall say,
"Hell today is vanquished, heaven is won today."

Venantius Fortunatus 530-609

These prophetic words, taken from a hymn of praise written long ago and later set to music from the fourteenth century, tell us many things. They predict that for centuries hence, people will still be looking for Heaven in their lives *and finding it*. And the reward for finding heaven is happiness.

I had a conversation with a friend on the subject of happiness, which culminated in the writing of this chapter. She was preparing a short wellness presentation on *the science of happiness*. In her preparations, she was faced with the question, "What is the difference between joy and happiness—or *is* there a difference?" She wanted my opinion on this. Interestingly, I had been thinking about the subject of happiness also, and here was an opportunity for the two of us to try to explore the answer together.

My initial response was that I truly believe joy is something that rises up from within—from our spirit. And that to find this organic joy we all have *naturally* within us, we may have to pass through awareness, truth or acknowledgement, *and* forgiveness. These are the methods we need to use to help us remove the negative energies we may be holding inside—negative energies that keep us from feeling joy. But what about happiness? Where does this come in?

What makes one person happy may not be the same for another, so happiness is perceived very individually. Yet, many stimulants seem to create similar temporary feelings of happiness in most people—like ice cream, for example—and obviously this reaction of happiness to the prospect of an ice cream treat arises from learned behaviour. According to Daniel Nettle, human beings are born with a present level of happiness that may fluctuate during their lives but remains basically unchanging[11]—not a pleasant thought for someone who is on the lower end of the happiness scale!

---

[11] Daniel Nettle, *Happiness: The Science behind Your Smile* (Oxford, England: Oxford University Press, 2005).

After much deliberation over what happiness is or isn't, here is where our discussion arrived: among other descriptors, could happiness simply be a state of mind—an attitude?

We thought about this for awhile, and unscientific as our discussion most certainly was, it did seem very plausible to us that happiness could be defined as a state of mind. I remembered an old Chinese proverb: "Your happiness is entwined with your outlook on life"—your attitude. If attitude is in any way related to one's ability to experience happiness, then most definitely it *can be cultivated* in those who do not normally grow it!

This represented an enormous breakthrough for both of us, each of whom has struggled to find happiness in our daily lives. And here is a very simple law in working with energy. When we engage in the pursuit of anything, it remains somewhere out there ahead of us like a carrot dangling on a long stick that is just out of our reach. We can see it. We occasionally feel it. But it doesn't allow us to catch up with it sufficiently *to live it* constantly. And so it remains a pursuit, and possibly even a struggle. It doesn't matter what it is we are pursuing. Happiness is no different.

To end the pursuit and to *engage* in happiness or any other quality of life or way of being, we must invite it into our daily life *to become us*, now. To do this, we take control of the stick that dangles the carrot. We remove the carrot and bring it into our hands and eventually into our mouths.

To conquer the carrot, we create a simple affirmation that is set in the present, not the future, as is a pursuit: *I welcome happiness into my life today*. And look at the words of the hymn above. This is actually an affirmation: "Welcome, happy morning!" And to this you may add two important words: "*with gratitude*." This suggests one's thanksgiving for something that is most assuredly happening today.

An affirmation of this nature is opening you up on an energy level to *engage* in happiness *today*. It is setting your mental compass towards learning a new way of responding and living—in happiness. It is changing the way you normally react. It is leading you into a new way of being. And in this sense, it is transforming you. The affirmation then changes to one of intent: "I am grateful to feel happiness."

And as you are transformed into a new way of being in which you *gratefully become happiness*, you are also now in full touch with your spirit, which is the source of the emotion of joy. It is at this point that mind and spirit come together, and happiness and joy converge. Affirmations are no longer required, for the feeling of happiness is now rising up from within you as *joy*. It no longer requires external coaching through the words of an affirmation.

According to author Marianne Williamson, we are happy to the extent that we choose to notice and create the reasons for happiness. She says that optimism and happiness are the results of spiritual work.[12] This should come

---

[12] Marianne Williamson, *A Year for Daily Wisdom* (Carlsbad, Calif.: Hay House, Inc, 1997), July 20.

as positive reinforcement to anyone who is desperately wanting to be happy and also attempting to find his or her spirit.

I am going to go out on a limb now and, contrary to Nettle's new scientific research, say that *happiness is something that anyone can achieve if he or she truly wants it.* It is something anyone can live and become if he or she chooses to do so. The world is filled with unhappy people. The world is filled with people who are unhappy because of so many reasons, all of which translate into the need for healing their lives. So, here is a prescription for healing: *Invite happiness into your life each day as a new way of living your life, and a new way of being!* And secondly: *Practise feeling happy by regularly exercising your authentic smile!*

Happiness is an espoused virtue. It is worth the search. Let's step back from the spiritual side of happiness for a moment and look at some interesting new information on this subject. Happiness research is now showing that despite the rising GNP in North America, people have not been getting significantly happier. In fact, economists are so concerned about this, the Gallup organization is developing a phone survey to measure national well-being in America, based on the work of happiness researchers![13]

A national conference held in Seattle in August 2005, called *Take Back Your Time*, challenged the notion that success should be primarily measured in economic terms and stated that work and life must be brought back into balance. The theory is that Americans are spending so much time in commuting to work as well as in work itself, that there simply isn't enough time left to connect with friends, spend time with family, or to simply relax— all "wellness" factors related to the experience of happiness.

It is extremely positive that economists are getting concerned about these issues. Finally, those who influence national policy decisions are paying attention to basic changes in societal values in an attempt to reclaim what has been lost through the explosive years of rapid economic growth. The economy may be healthier, but the people are not. And this has been reflected in something called *happiness* as a measure of well-being, marked against the GNP. The prospects of this are exciting.

It doesn't take a scientist to understand how the lack of happiness in one's life feels. We all know what it feels like when we are unhappy. The message to receive from all of this is that if we want to be *happy as a way of being*, we must take a look at our lifestyle and be prepared to make changes.

Research has shown a direct link between positive emotion and the strength of the immune system. Becoming happy as a way of being, therefore, cannot be overlooked by anyone who is interested in his or her health. One's genetic makeup is always a fundamental influence in the risk factors for disease in anyone's life; but a positive emotional state of well-being cannot be ruled out as a defiant attempt at prevention.

---

[13] Cascadia Scorecard Weblog (Northwest Environment Watch's take on the news that really matters), January 11, 2005.

So if the daily commute is beginning to take its toll on you by robbing you of precious time from those people and activities that bring you happiness, then it's time to look at making some changes in your life. Or if your work is demanding more hours than are humanly acceptable, then perhaps it is time to look for a new job. Or if you are unhappy with yourself because of insufficient attention to your physical body—like an unhealthy weight, for example—perhaps it's time to do something concrete and positive to make meaningful change there as well. The choice is always yours to make. The important aspect in all of this is that you become aware of what you have in your life, what is missing, and what you need to do to find happiness.

Happiness Is a Chosen Way of Being!

Happiness is not a commodity that can be purchased through an expensive lifestyle. Happiness is a way of being—a particular kind of goodness—that seems to emanate from a spirit that has been allowed to free itself from harmful mental attitudes and beliefs, and thus to express itself in all ways humanly possible.

Back to the words of the hymn: "Hell today is vanquished, heaven is won today," and the chapter "The Dark Night of the Soul," as we become *happy as a way of being*, we find Heaven. We release ourselves from a living Hell. The words *Heaven and Hell* cease to describe an illusive place that mystically exists high above us or deep below us. Instead, Heaven and Hell can be viewed as words that describe a state of being that we impose upon ourselves—as a choice—in terms of the way we *choose* to live our lives.

To release oneself from an existence of Hell is to put an end to the struggle that has become one's life. Outer struggle may be the commute or the long hours at work, while inner struggle may be the torment we experience or the flagellation we inflict upon ourselves for the way things in our lives are or aren't or haven't been. So, we attempt to introduce appropriate changes that will eliminate the outer struggle. And we summon up the inner strength and courage to find a better way to perceive our lives and ourselves.

Here is another opportunity to use affirmations. Begin by saying the words, "Welcome, happy morning!" And then reaffirm these words moment to moment as you go through your morning, each time you feel yourself digressing from this new way of being. Next, the words become, "Welcome, happy afternoon!" as you proceed into the afternoon, and later, "Welcome, happy evening!"

What happens as a result of all of this positive affirming? You put yourself in touch with your inner spirit! You will feel a sense of something more in your life, perhaps for the first time. Here you will rest long enough to drink in this new feeling and express heartfelt gratitude for the feeling. From there, you gradually approach the threshold of Heaven. And what follows this foretaste of Heaven is an awareness of what life *can* be for the choosing. And because you have engaged your spirit, your spirit will then take over. It will lead you (possibly through your dark night) into *happiness as a way of being*. But first, there will be many stops along the way, for you will have engaged in your own healing process.

I have already spoken about the healing process and the need to release or discharge negative energy from our bodies and minds. It is the release of negativity that allows us to hold on to this new way of being and is an essential part of our healing. And here is a new piece of information: *We are the creators of how we will move through our own healing journey.*

We can look to the words of Isaiah 40: 4, set to the beautiful music of *The Messiah,*[14] as a guide to our healing journey: "Every valley shall be exalted, every mountain made low, the crooked straight and the rough places plain." Presumably, if we allow ourselves to follow our spirit, these are the things that will happen. If we choose to ignore our spirit, then the valley shall remain low, the mountain shall remain high, the path crooked, and the terrain rugged.

We ignore our spirit when we resist letting go of control by our mind. To fully engage in spiritual direction, we must relinquish this mental control and surrender to our spiritual direction or guidance. Only then will the crooked path be made straight for us and the rugged terrain become smooth. Only then will the negative energy we hold in our bodies become transformed into positive, life-affirming, healthy energy.

Let Happiness Empower You to Heal and Release!

We enter the healing process reliving all the awful things that have happened to us. They have become a part of who we are and will always remain as part of our past; we cannot escape this. But as we bring ourselves to our own healing, we may or may not choose a mindset of welcoming happiness into our day.

For those who have been severely traumatized by life, it may seem unthinkable to suggest that for each day of their healing journey they invite happiness into their lives for that day. And it may seem even more illogical to suggest that they give thanks for the blessings flowing into their lives, yet this may be the only way one can approach each day when the need for healing is so intense.

With each new day, we have the opportunity to welcome Heaven into our lives as we make our way out of our dark night—the place called Hell, filled with crooked pathways and rugged terrain—as we release the negative energy we have inside of us.

And if we continue to think about our healing journey as a trip we are taking, with many stopovers and sights to see, we begin to regard our journey

---

[14] George Frederick Handel, *The Messiah,* "Ev'ry valley shall be exalted" (written and first performed in Dublin, Ireland, in 1742).

with renewed vision. We can make the trip long or short, by staying as long as we want at each of the places we need to stop.

We can begin each day of our trip dreading the day's events and hiding behind our fears—afraid to look at the sights; or we may begin each day refreshed as we welcome the beauty of the new day into our lives. Thus we strengthen ourselves to be able to face, see, and acknowledge what must be faced, seen, and acknowledged before we can leave this place and progress to the next stopover.

This puts an entirely new spin on one's healing process. It explains why some people never progress in their healing journey and seem to become victimized by it all. Yet others seem to go through it more quickly. Knowing that we have at least this much control in our lives removes the tendency to feel victimized, thus shortening the dark night, or even skirting its edges.

Each day of the journey is really an opportunity. Every moment of each day of the journey creates an opening for us to welcome happiness into our life and to express gratitude for what hasn't even transpired yet. Beginning each day with a positive mindset creates inner strength. It connects us with our spirit, which in turn connects us with the strength we receive from the Universe, from God. It provides the necessary courage to face whatever presents itself throughout the day—even during the long commute!

And from moment to moment each day, we draw on this divine inner strength with both gratitude and happiness. The knowledge and sensation of one's inner strength may be the *only* thing in any moment that *can* be associated with either gratitude or happiness—but the point is, in any given moment, *they can be found*!

By retraining our minds to find and acknowledge gratitude and happiness within the moment that we need inner strength, our strength is instantly renewed—our Hell is vanquished and our Heaven is found! *We gain new strength, we mount up with wings like eagles, we run and do not get tired, we walk and do not get weary.*[15]

And step by step, we progress on our healing journey. We are able to move through the obstacles to inner silence and peace more easily because we have engaged the light of our inner spirit to help us find our way out through all the darkness, on the best route possible. We have conquered our own symbolic death on the cross of torture by resurrecting our spirit from the torments of our depths. From this point onward, our mind and spirit work together to make the journey easier for both; and through this inner harmony our body is strengthened also.

One step at a time, we alter our attitude through a deliberate mindset of happiness. We bring the joy that is so available to us within our spirit out into our daily lives, making it fully operative . . . able to bring us back home to ourselves again . . . allowing us to find the divinity—Heaven—that resides *within* ourselves . . . allowing us to find divinity in *all that is*.

---

[15] Isaiah 40: 31.

When we have reached this stage—and it *is* possible to reach this stage—we are in a wonderful position to do the spirit's work. We are capable of assisting others to facilitate their own healing process. It is here that the divinity of man may be found and exercised within *ordinary* lives.

For one who finds his happiness and his joy within himself and within himself finds light as well, is at one with God.

Krishna

For the record . . .

Finding happiness is not about living one's life in a state of bliss, or suddenly becoming an extravert in all of one's relationships with people. Nor do these ways of being necessarily follow the uncovering of one's own spirituality.

Nor is the finding of happiness about never having to face challenging times, or stressful times, or sad and difficult times. Finding happiness within one's life is simply part of one's ability to experience a sense of wholeness. And wholeness of body, mind, and spirit represents a unity of these three aspects of our being—what I refer to as the Holy Trinity of one's being—that allows for optimum functionality of the body, mind, and spirit working together in complete harmony. Experiencing wholeness is the goal of opening to your inner spirit and then surrendering to its guidance.

It is because of our ability to surrender to our spirit's guidance that we are able to make contact with the wisdom that is in our soul. This is the wisdom that has accumulated during the millennia of our being, which forms both the mystery and the true identity of who we really are.

When we experience wholeness, we are able to bring ourselves completely to everything we do, with our full physical energy, clarity of mind, and spiritual guidance. With all three aspects of our being functioning harmoniously, we can achieve meaningful living within each day of our lives. This is the meaning of wholeness as it pertains to our spirituality. It is the state of mind that we reach when we physically, mentally, and emotionally surrender to our spirit—when we are resurrected from the depths of our inner torment to the light and love of life.

Within this kind of living, joy and happiness are naturally present. And peace that is beyond all understanding follows.

This is the meaning of human divinity.

How wonderful the day when all *would rejoice and be glad in it!*

Commentary on Psalms 118: 24

EIGHT

THE ALCHEMY OF GRATITUDE

It is your conscious spiritual awareness that allows you to alter your attitude from negative to positive on a moment-to-moment basis.

Of all the various energy-type healing modalities that exist, there is probably none more simple or effective than the practice of gratitude. Like happiness, gratitude—for those who practise it continuously—becomes *a way of being*. Gratitude creates a positive spin to any situation. It is this positive spin on the mind, body, emotions, and spirit that transforms its users.

Not only can gratitude transform the individual who practises it regularly, it can positively impact those who come in contact with that individual! It rubs off, having a temporary impact at least, on the person who encounters it.

Among other identifiers, gratitude is a form of acknowledgement to one who has either done something for you or who has given you something. This acknowledgement is a form of positive energy exchange that is felt by the one on the receiving end as well as yourself. Without its expression, there is an energy void.

For those who struggle with their own negative issues—not seeing opportunities to express gratitude for their lives—it is easy to fall back into negative ways again after being with someone who practises gratitude as a way of being. It is easy to dismiss the positive ways of the person who exhibits gratitude as: "She's special," or "He was born that way," or "I could never be like that."

What do I mean by practising gratitude as *a way of being*? I mean that I learn to find gratitude in every experience that comes my way. And in finding gratitude, I become aware of this new experience of feeling a positive energy flow within my being.

It is this positive energy flow that renders gratitude as a most effective energy-healing modality. It is like retrofitting your current attitudes and behaviours with new and positive approaches and thus learning to respond to situations in positive ways.

There is a spiritual precept within the practice of Reiki—an energy-healing modality—that says, "Show gratitude to every living thing." It is an effective precept when used, because it reminds its user to find opportunities to practise gratitude towards every living creature and human that comes her way each day—whether it is one's pet, someone else's pet, a member of the family, a next-door neighbour, or a bird that lands on the branch of a tree outside your window.

Approaching a neighbour from the perspective of gratitude renders a very different encounter than when approaching him or her with indifference. It softens the interchange. It allows a positive flow of energy into your system and impacts the outcome of the experience.

To explain, simply, how gratitude can affect one's life, we will look at something that affects everyone—eating! But, to begin with, we have to have food to prepare. So this gratitude practice is going to begin at home with a character named Sam, who is a faithful practitioner of gratitude, and who is presently going through his cupboards making a grocery-shopping list.

By way of introduction, Sam is one of those people you just love to be around. He is warm and sensitive. He seems happy most of the time and can bring you out of the doldrums by his very presence. He is, by nature, an extravert. Sam lives in suburbia of Any City, North America.

Sam has many choices of grocery stores in which he can shop. They all carry fresh and frozen produce, canned and dry goods, dairy products, meat and fish of all types, eggs, as well as multiple varieties of treats, plus breads and cereals, etc.—all the usual grocery store items we find in North American stores. Let's look in at Sam's weekly trek to the grocery store.

Before Sam goes grocery shopping each Saturday morning, he checks his cupboards and refrigerator to see what he needs. While he is doing this, he is filled with feelings of gratitude for his home, his family, for whom he is shopping, and his freedom to be able to go out to shop at any time that is convenient for him—for there is at least one store that has exceptionally long hours, perhaps even overnight shopping availability. Sam is fully aware and mindful that his physical health and abilities allow him to independently get to the store to do his shopping; and for all of this, he says an inner word of thanks *every day*.

Sam has a love affair with food. This is not to say that Sam overeats. In fact, Sam is very careful about what types of food he eats and how much. Sam is very aware that to maintain his continuing good health, he must eat a variety of fresh and wholesome foods that are prepared carefully to preserve their nutrients, flavour, and colour, etc. This food awareness is what contributes to Sam's love affair with food. He not only enjoys the eating of it, he enjoys the journey he takes with it to get it to the table—the buying and the preparation and, finally, the serving of it.

Presently, though, Sam is still searching his cupboards. His mind is taking note of what he needs to buy, based on his earlier chat with his wife, and it is dancing ahead to what different meals they might create together in the coming week. And all the while, Sam is feeling happy inside. He is aware of how fortunate he is to be able to do all of this, and he is grateful. He pauses a moment to take it all in—to truly feel and breathe through his gratitude—then, with a smile on his face and a song in his heart, he is off to shop.

Sam climbs into his van, which needs to be washed; he decides to stop for gas and a wash on his way to the store. He turns on the radio and sings along. Shortly, he arrives at the gas station, gets out and serves himself gas, then proceeds to pay and get his van wash ticket, greeting the sleepy teenager behind the counter with an energetic "Good morning!" Back in his van now, there is a lineup for the wash, as he had anticipated, so he picks up the newspaper from the seat beside him to read while waiting for his turn.

Underneath the newspaper is one of Sam's children's toys that must have fallen out of her backpack the day before. Sam smiles as he looks at it and thinks about how much his daughter loves this toy. And then he thinks about how much he loves his daughter. And then he thinks about how much he loves his entire family—his daughter, his son, and his wife, and how much he is *in love* with her. And a shiver of thankfulness runs through his body. He turns again to his newspaper, and before he knows it, his turn has come. Just a couple of minutes in the wash now, and he is on his way to the grocery store!

Along the way, there is a traffic slowdown. It is Saturday morning and it seems that, like Sam, a lot of people are out early doing errands. He looks up at the beautiful morning sky while his car is idling in traffic, waiting for the light to change, and he breathes in another breath of joy in being alive on this beautiful morning. He thinks about his family again. He is so proud of them and so unbelievably happy to be sharing his life with all of them.

The light changes, and Sam is off down the road still humming along to the radio and thinking good thoughts. He turns into the parking lot of the grocery store, parks, and heads off into the store. He treats himself to a fresh cup of coffee that awaits him just inside the door, and sips it with pleasure while he fills his cart with the items on his mental list. He stops to chat with the familiar face behind the meat counter, and exchanges light and happy banter. He moves about the store with ease and eventually arrives at the checkout about the time his coffee cup is almost empty.

Through the checkout now, he winks at the middle-aged woman serving him, and calls her by the name on her tag as he wishes her a good day. Back to the van, he carefully loads his bags of groceries, puts his cart away, and climbs back into the van to drive home. But before he does, he calls his wife on his cell phone to see if there is anything she would like him to pick up on his way home.

When Sam gets home, his children are both up. He squats down and hugs them close to him when he comes through the door. He asks them to come out and help him to carry in the groceries and to help put them away. They enjoy doing this because Daddy always brings them a treat from the grocery store on Saturday mornings.

And he brings Mommy a treat, too. Today, it was fresh tulips that he selected for her in the fresh flower case. Sam's wife, Elizabeth, accepts the tulips lovingly and gives Sam a big hug and a moist kiss to show her appreciation. Sam feels like he is floating now as he goes back outside to put the van in the garage. He is in love with his family and with his life. He is filled with awareness of gratitude.

Sam's story of eating doesn't end here. Sam and Elizabeth will share in the preparation of the food throughout the week. Sam's children will set the table for their evening meals together. The tulips will form the centrepiece this week so that everyone can enjoy them. And the children will take turns lighting the family dinner candle, under supervision.

And each evening, before the meal is consumed, Sam will lead his family in words of thanksgiving, allowing each person a moment to add their special word of thanks for what happened to him or her during the day.

During the meal, Sam and Elizabeth will engage their children in conversation they can understand and in which they can participate. When the meal is over, another moment will be spent in thanksgiving before each person shares in the removal of dishes from the table and in the cleanup, each shouldering his or her individual responsibility.

After kitchen cleanup, Sam and Elizabeth will have their coffee together alone in the living room while the children work on their homework or have some quiet time reading or playing in their rooms. This is the time that Sam and his wife reserve to be alone together. And during this time, both Sam and Elizabeth will take great care to truly listen to one another and to show interest in what the other is saying.

So this is basically how Sam lives his life. "Is Sam *real*?" you may ask. "Can anyone ever live a life like Sam lives?" What do you think? *Imagine for a moment that you are Sam.* And be honest in this little test. In which aspects of Sam's trip to the grocery store do you see yourself reacting differently from Sam? And when Sam arrived back home, which parts of the story do not fit with your own reality? Then ask yourself the following question: "Why *can't* Sam's story be true?"

"Why *can't* Sam's story be true?"

Think about this for a few minutes. Think about *Sam's reality*. Try to visualize how it would *feel* to live Sam's reality. How does it make *you* feel when you think about your own reality versus Sam's reality? Is there a difference? Is Sam's reality healthy? *Why? Or why not?*

Because the subject of this chapter is the alchemy of gratitude, it is obvious that the story of Sam is being used to graphically portray what living a life of gratitude *can* actually mean. Sam may appear to be just a happy-go-lucky guy. But look again. Sam consciously takes time throughout his day to acknowledge his gratitude. He does not take anything for granted.

Even when he is alone, Sam's thoughts are positive. He plans his day carefully. He thinks ahead and prepares himself with a newspaper in case he has to wait at the car wash. This prevents him from being stressed by the lineup. He chooses to enjoy his surroundings while he waits in traffic rather than being stressed by the delay. He hums along with the music on the van radio and takes in the beauty of the morning sky.

He treats himself to a cup of coffee and remembers to get something special for each family member. Sam is very calculating in all his behaviours. He is definitely not a happy-go-lucky guy. But, he is definitely a happy guy! And he is training his children also to live a life of gratitude. He gives them responsibilities and he gives them rewards. He encourages them to participate in discussion around the dinner table at night, and to speak about those things for which they are grateful.

He sets aside time to be alone with his wife. And, as we can see from his grocery trek, Sam also sets aside time to be alone with himself. All of these things make his life easier. They allow positive interaction with his children and with his wife. They allow positive interaction with complete strangers. They allow a positive flow of energy within his body and mind in all of his activities. And those who share Sam's life feel his positive flow of energy.

Sam's reality in the grocery store scenario is continued when he goes to work. He treats his co-workers with respect; he remembers names; he listens; he opens doors for others; he says "thank you" to people who do something kind or helpful; he willingly makes a fresh pot of coffee when he takes the last cup; and so on. He is an all-around "nice guy"—the kind of person you would like as a co-worker, a friend, a father, a husband.

Sam's life is one of high energy—not the frenetic kind of high energy, but rather the smooth, calm, and steady energy that comes from a continuous contact with the loving, positive flow of the divine energy of his spirit. For Sam is definitely in touch with his spirit *all the time*. And even if Sam has an occasional negative thought, he is so accustomed to a way of being that is filled with gratitude, he is able to quickly alter his attitude to "the positive" again.

And herein lies the secret to living a life of gratitude. It is all about *consciously* making a decision *each day* and about *each issue* that comes along that has the potential for letting negativity into your life. At the very moment the issue presents itself, you learn to *alter your attitude in that moment*.

This means that you do not spend even one ounce of energy thinking about the issue in a negative way. Instead, you allow yourself to look for the positive. And in finding the positive, you stimulate a positive flow of energy into your being. It is your conscious awareness that allows you to alter your attitude from negative to positive on a moment-to-moment basis.

Is this easy to do? Again, what do you think? It is actually quite tough to switch from dismay or antagonism to gratitude when confronted by a display of someone else's foolish or provocative behaviour. But when the incident is over, that is the time to make the switch.

Rather than focusing on the event now past, allow yourself instead to switch over to whatever positive aspect of the situation you can find—possibly just that it is now over! You may need to debrief, to talk the incident out with someone else, in order to help you release the feelings it has created within you.

As you are able to release this negative energy from your being, you can reconnect with your positive flow of energy from your spirit once again. It is here in the quiet of positive energy flow that you will be guided to know what to do, if there is a need for action on your part.

To hold onto the memory of the incident and the way it has made you feel as it was occurring is to cut you off from your positive spiritual energy and to disengage any opportunity to find gratitude or any opportunity to allow healing to occur within your own being as a result of the incident.

When you are caught up in traumatizing situations—of someone else's anger, for example—you are inundated with their negative energy, which must be released as quickly as possible. Otherwise, it settles inside of you and is felt as an emotional assault on your system, with physical consequences. If you yourself have unresolved issues with anger, you will probably feel the effect of this emotion somewhere in your body.

It is important to be aware of exactly where in your body you feel this assault. It will provide information for you about your own health and potential for health-related problems in the part of your body where you hold negative energy.

It is very possible that if a person has a buildup—over time—of negative emotion in the body that is felt in the chest, for example, he may be at risk of developing some form of illness in that same part of his body or that is controlled by that part of his body. This statement is based on an ancient Eastern theory that is slowly beginning to make itself known in the West. It suggests that energy-centre function, or chakra system function, is directly related to health disorders.

So, to work with our example, if negative energy accumulates in the chest area—the heart chakra or energy centre—weakness of the heart, lungs, circulatory system, thoracic spine, or shoulders may develop if the individual is unable to release this negative energy from his body and mind. And if the person's familial medical history shows problems in any of these areas, his vulnerability increases. Many books exist on the chakra system and this "old world" approach to medical issues that are both fascinating and educational to read.

You might want to take a few minutes now to consider why you spend any time at all thinking "bad thoughts" about people or situations. And further, why do you have trouble letting this type of behaviour go?

Recognize also the energy you consume by spending time in negative ways, and the effect negativity has on you physically, mentally, emotionally, and spiritually. It is rather like the quest for happiness. We prevent ourselves from feeling gratitude or happiness by victimizing ourselves and *choosing* to remain in this role!

Are you willing to *try* another way? This is part of your own inner healing. It is not healthy to hold on to bad thoughts about people. Instead, try to understand that what they represent for you is the need for healing around the issues they remind you of.

Inner Healing

When we engage in the alchemy of gratitude, we realize that the entire world becomes our mirror. All of the experiences we have that create a negative reaction within us show us something about ourselves that needs to be healed—for this is the way universal life energy works.

It also shows us the need for another's healing. But since we are all spiritual beings living our independent human adventure, we need to remember that we all have choices about how we will live within the physical dimension.

If we have been exposed to an upsetting incident that someone else has created, it is really a lesson for *all* those who witness it—and in particular, oneself. Something is to be learned from it. Inner healing is necessary if we have felt personally assaulted by it. And in this, gratitude can be found—for the incident is showing us an energy pattern we need to release within ourselves.

What follows then is the release itself through tears or talk or writing . . . Or you may have a terrible feeling inside your gut or chest that is emotionally based and seems to get bigger and bigger until it bursts through some form of acknowledgement you are able to make in relation to what needs to be healed within you.

And sometimes release will be subtle, occurring slowly—bit by bit—over a long period of time. Eventually, with the full release, you will be changed. You will have become transformed. It may take moments to months for this to happen. It all depends upon how much of this form of negative energy you hold within you and how willing you are to let it go . . .

Remember how you feel when you are with someone who is positive and whose way of being is that of gratitude? Would you like to be able to hold on to the positive way you *feel about yourself* when you are with this person? The good news is that you can! *You, too, can live a life of gratitude.*

It may take quite a bit of practice, but you can start any time you wish. And the guarantee for adopting this altered way of being is that you will definitely notice a change in the way you feel. *You will have more energy and you will actually be able to experience a sense of inner peace!* This is because you will have tapped into your *spiritual* energy source. You will have stopped the drain of energy that happens when you engage in negative thinking and behaviours or when you are caught in someone else's negative energy trap.

And, over time, your life will become transformed into a *new way of being*. You will more easily be able to find the silver lining in all the clouds that come into your life. And you will even be grateful for those clouds!

And the final alchemical reaction of your transformation is the impact you will have on others. People (and animals) will feel your positive flow of spiritual energy. They will be attracted to it. They may even attempt to emulate your ways in an attempt to be this way themselves. You are helping to transform humanity to a new way of being, by being that way yourself!

Let's return again to Sam.

Is It Possible to Find Sam's Reality?

Would you like to have Sam as a friend? A father? A husband? A teacher? A boss at work?

It *is* possible to find Sam's reality! It *is* possible to live Sam's reality! It *is* possible to be transformed to a new way of being! Let's take a closer look at how Sam's transformation occurred.

First of all, as Sam began his practice of gratitude, it was like a revelation to him that there was another way of viewing his life. Things he had previously taken for granted now loomed dramatically on the horizon. He became interested in the subtleties of life that he had never even considered before—things like the beauty found throughout nature, and his ability to experience this beauty through each of his senses.

He began to understand the concept of energy that pervades nature and creation itself. As part of this new awareness, he became aware of his own energy and began to speculate on those things that detracted from his energy or increased it. And as a part of all this, he became aware of the people in his life and the activities that impacted his energy level.

Gradually, Sam became aware of all the areas where he was investing in negative energy—energy that was draining his system, sometimes leaving him feeling tired and devoid of the energy to do all the things he wanted to do.

He still *did* these things, and the activities helped to revive him, but he could not shake the dullness or heaviness he felt inside of himself at times. He had a medical checkup and all his blood work was "negative," which meant that everything was within normal limits. His doctor was unable to find any discernable reason for Sam's periodic low energy.

Meanwhile, Sam became very interested in his diet, thinking *this* may be the cause of his low energy. Perhaps he wasn't eating the right kind of foods. He searched the Internet for nutritional sites that would teach him improved ways of maximizing food choices and getting the most nutritional value from food.

He subscribed to a nutritional magazine, and picked up some healthy living cookbooks. And through his research and subsequent learning, he made changes to his diet and discovered a new interest in the preparation of food.

This new interest stimulated creative energy within him as he engaged in shopping experiences in various supermarkets, farmer's markets, specialty shops, and health food stores—places he hardly knew existed previously. It became exciting for him. And with the excitement, his energy increased.

He was beginning to feel better. But still, there were times when he would awaken in the morning feeling just as tired as when he went to bed. After one such morning, he began to worry about his health again, and returned to his doctor to see if there wasn't something wrong with him—some tumour growing silently perhaps, depriving him of the new energy he had found. Again, his doctor reassured him with more tests and further examination, that there was nothing physiological to be found as the cause of his periodic low energy.

Sam left the doctor's office feeling relieved and somewhat excited by the prospect that maybe he was searching in the wrong area to find the source of his low energy. If it wasn't physical, could it be emotional? Could it be that he was letting things bother him to such a degree that they were affecting his energy level? And if this was so, what *were* these things?

Still, in his daily gratitude practice, Sam went through his usual morning mantra of saying "thank you" to the universe for all of the blessings in his life. And then he changed his routine and began to say thank you for the energy he felt when he was feeling grateful for his life.

And *then* he said, "Thank you for showing me what I still need to understand that will help me to feel more energy." This was the ticket! This was the way to finding the final cause of his energy drain! He had discovered how to manifest solutions to problems by engaging the universe in helping him to find the answers he needed!

This use of "futuristic gratitude" creates an opening for gratitude to be found in the future and, in this case, to resolve a problem. And in creating this opening, the alchemical forces available in the universe were able to become active within Sam.

He didn't have any answer yet, but he had a very strong feeling that he was on the verge of learning something about himself that he needed to know—information that would help him to feel more energized and able to hold his energy.

In the excitement he felt from his breakthrough in discovering futuristic gratitude, Sam dressed in his best suit and tie and went whistling off to work, feeling very exhilarated. He stopped at a favourite coffee shop to pick up his usual cup of coffee before going to the office.

He emerged from the elevator still feeling the wonderful "high" that comes from anticipation. He turned to wave "Good morning" to one of his co-workers and missed seeing the person who was in his pathway; he bumped into her before he could move out of her way.

The coffee flew out of his hand and onto the floor, creating an enormous splash and sending the coffee up both of his pant legs and onto his jacket and tie. It also splashed the woman!

She was furious and began to yell and curse at him. And instinctively, Sam yelled and cursed back at her. There was so much yelling that people came out of their cubicles to see what was going on. The woman would not stop berating Sam about the foolishness of the accident.

All Sam heard was *accident*. He really felt that there were no accidents in life, but rather, there were incidents that occurred to teach you something. Holding this belief enabled him to put an end to the yelling on both their parts. He took a deep breath to still his anger. "I'm terribly sorry," he said to the woman in a now quiet and controlled voice.

"Why didn't you say that in the first place?" she responded indignantly, as she wiped away at the coffee stain on her dress, almost in tears now. "You'll pay for my dry cleaning bill," she added, regaining her former hostility.

"I will be happy to do that for you," Sam said, quietly. "Again, I'm terribly sorry. It was foolish of me. I wasn't looking where I was going."

Sam looked down at his own clothes and realized he had to go home and change. As he was on his way back down the elevator, the words *I have to go home and change* went over and over in his mind. Obviously there was some symbolic significance here. What did these words mean beyond the obvious change of clothes? How was *he* to change?

By the time he got back home and had changed into clean clothing, he realized what he had never understood about himself. He had a quick temper. He had instantly lashed out at the woman whom he had bumped into at the office when she criticized him for not looking where he was going.

And then his mind flashed back over other scenarios in his life where his temper had gotten the better of him. He had actually lost friends over silly incidents that he had made worse through his inappropriate, hot-tempered reaction.

He began to realize that he truly did need to change. He needed to change a lot. Could this have been the understanding he had given thanks for earlier this morning? Was this the way answers came when he worked with the universe—by spilling coffee over his best suit and falling out with a beautiful woman who because of it would probably never look at him again?

In his resolve to get to the bottom of his quest, he decided that perhaps this was at least part of the answer he was looking for. Perhaps he needed to watch his temper and control his anger. But what did that have to do with his energy level? He certainly had used up a lot of energy over this incident and the ensuing anger that he had felt both at the woman as well as himself. He felt drained by the time he had changed his clothing and started back on the freeway to return to work. And perhaps, when one is so easily prone to anger, one's energy is impacted because of this. Certainly, he thought, his energy would be different from that of someone who reacts to situations calmly and sees no reason to be angry—the same situations that create anger within himself. Perhaps there was a relationship between always being on edge emotionally, and the potential for energy drain because of this. Quite obviously,

Sam now realized, a calm and peaceful person preserves his energy very simply by the way in which he thinks and reacts and perceives.

And then Sam let his memory zero in on those times in his past where he reacted to situations in anger. He had never felt there was anything abnormal about his reactions. But as he reviewed these situations now as objectively as he could, he realized that there was another way he might have reacted— another way that would have left him without feelings of guilt and remorse afterwards, feelings that never seemed to get resolved. And perhaps this was what was really behind his energy drain: the unresolved issues that were created as a result of his hot temper and the resulting fallout from his anger . . . each issue with its own little funnel siphoning off Sam's precious energy.

And just as quickly as he had gained this insight in his relationship to his energy loss, he remembered the incident from earlier this morning and he reacted angrily all over again! "Damn," he thought. "Why did this have to happen today of all days? Why didn't that woman see me coming and move out of my way? Why was it supposed to be my fault? She wasn't watching where she was going either!"

In his renewed anger, Sam began to drive faster. He took his eyes away from the road ahead for a moment as he searched for his cell phone to call his office. With all of the excitement in the office earlier, he had forgotten that he had a meeting that would be beginning at this very moment. Furiously, he dialed the first three digits before looking up again to make certain there were no traffic obstacles.

But it was too late. The traffic had slowed and Sam hadn't. He managed to brake sufficiently to reduce the impact as he smashed into the vehicle in front of him. His first thought during the impact was once again that of anger.

"This can't be happening! I have no time for this!" Sam yelled at the top of his voice.

And then he let out another yell at the traffic backup and the car ahead of him and swore at the situation and the black day that this was turning out to be. And as if he had someone sitting in the seat next to him, once again he heard the words, *I have to change.*

There was no person sitting there. The words were coming from inside of Sam. Here and now, *he had a chance to change—in that very moment.* He surveyed his vehicle and himself. He wasn't hurt. He got out of the car and went quickly to check on the driver of the car in front of him.

She appeared to be uninjured, but the back of her car was. It would take thousands of dollars in Sam's insurance to repair the damage. His insurance costs would be rising dramatically because of it. And Sam's front end would also need repair. Sam took all of this in, in an instant.

"Are you all right, Miss?" he inquired as he opened the woman's car door, hardly recognizing the sound of his own voice that had switched from a volume and tone of anger to the quiet and caring words of concern.

She looked into his kind eyes and said, "Yes, I am fine. I saw you coming. I braced myself and I prayed for us both," she said. "I think it might have been worse if I hadn't."

Sam was shocked by her answer and surprised that instead of her being angry, she was speaking with gratitude. *It could have been worse*, she was saying. She wasn't angry with him, nor was she angry at the accident!

And there was that word again—*accident*. Twice in one day. He obviously needed reinforcement to learn what he needed to learn. Here was his second "opportunity." And already he was playing it differently. He was aware of the opportunity aspect of this accident—an opportunity to react differently in situations that normally would cause him to erupt in anger.

"May I call someone for you?" Sam offered. "Your car can't be driven like this, I'm afraid."

Then Sam called the highway patrol. When the young woman told him there was no one to call, he offered to drive her home after the police were finished with their investigation. She accepted.

Sam had a lot to think about after all this was over. He had begun his day with futuristic gratitude through his desire to be shown what was leaving him with reduced energy.

He had his first epiphany in hearing the words *I have to change*. But even with this information and his ability to link his coffee spill accident to his hot temper, he fell back into his usual ways of becoming angry all over again.

And it was his anger that led to Sam's second accident of the day—an accident that could have been very serious, but miraculously was not. Instead, through his interaction with the young woman he rear-ended, he had learned something more about gratitude. He learned that gratitude can become a way of being. Gratitude can create a positive reaction to any situation and transform its user . . . for in that moment, Sam did feel transformed.

Sam had learned that it is possible to react with gratitude rather than anger when you have an accident. It was a teaching he would never forget. Nor would he ever forget the young woman who taught him. Her name was Elizabeth.

Joy is to see God in everything.

Julian of Norwich, 14th century.

NINE

SIMPLIFYING LIFE

I've been running since I was a child,
Some would call this freedom,
Some would call it wild.

Unknown

I have reserved this chapter till almost the end for a very good reason. Without an awareness and understanding of some of the things in life that challenge us, and without an opportunity to learn new ways of dealing with life's challenges, it is tough to simplify our life such that we begin to brake for butterflies.

There is an allegory in *The Teaching of Buddha*[16] that talks about a man who set out on a journey one day, and in the course of his travels he had to cross a river. With no bridge in sight, he built himself a raft. The raft served him well, and he safely made his way across the river. When he reached the other side, he wondered what he would do with this raft. Should he leave it on the riverbank to rot, or should he carry it with him in case he might have to use it again? The man made the decision to carry it with him. The teaching of Buddha thus states that such a decision represents an encumbrance—a burden—that this man will continue to carry as long as he keeps the now useless raft. It has served the purpose for which it was built; it is no longer useful as he now walks along the footpaths of his journey.

This simple teaching is designed to make us consider all the rafts we may be carrying with us in life that no longer serve us in a useful way. All we need to do is to look around our homes or our offices to see any number of superfluous "rafts" lying about. What do these encumbrances do to our own journey of life? How do they impede us? *Do* they impede us? Are they an unnecessary burden that we can now live without? Are they taking up space within an already determined or perhaps crowded way of living? Do they represent a need to simplify the way we live our lives?

---

[16] Bukkyo Dendo Kyokai, *The Teaching of Buddha* (Tokyo: Kosaido Printing Co., Ltd., 1966).

In the chapter you have just read, Sam and Elizabeth have certainly learned to simplify their lives. Otherwise, they could never live the way they do. They would never be able to sit down with their family at the dinner table each night, as an example, because one or another would be running out the door to the next activity of the day.

Evening is a time at Sam and Elizabeth's home when they protect their family time. Following a day filled with activities at school or at work, they use the evening as a time to gear down, to share in household responsibilities and to relax after their mutually busy days.

Sam and Elizabeth are teaching their children to take time to look after themselves, to experience some "downtime" as a routine each day after school. They have searched out extracurricular children's activities for them to do on Saturday, thereby guarding weeknight time for homework, outdoor play and exercise, relaxation, light chores, and family interaction. This formula for living will remain with these children throughout their school years and probably throughout their lives.

Sam and Elizabeth have learned to simplify their lives. Their lives are in balance! Again, you might think that Sam and Elizabeth's lifestyle is completely unrealistic in today's busy world, and that in order to get ahead, children and adults need to use every moment of the waking day to be doing something that will help them meet this objective.

But take another look. Each member of this family is getting everything done that needs to be done. And, they are getting it done well, happily, stress-free and with full family support. Chances are very good that they will each accomplish as much as or more than someone who undertakes too many activities at all times.

At some point, the need for rest and relaxation catches up to those who take on too much. Usually they get sick with a cold or the flu; finally, their body and mind have a chance to rest! When people are constantly on the go, they are less able to consciously connect with their spiritual self or to hear their inner guidance. So, with a tired body and mind and a potentially disconnected or suppressed spirit, their life gets completely out of balance.

Perhaps life just gets simpler all by itself as we get older and as we develop more mature attitudes towards life in general. But this statement doesn't help a young person in his or her prime, who would dearly love life to be simpler. For these young people, life can be extremely stressful. With youth on their side, they naturally have more energy to cope with life's stressors. But that energy can eventually be usurped when there is no break from life's demands.

Middle-aged people also experience stress in their lives as they find themselves sandwiched between the demands of their children and the increasing needs and dependencies of their parents. And for them to be able to cope with all of it at a time when their career is at its peak, they must learn to simplify the way they live their lives.

Let's take a look now at some of the influences in society that serve to complicate our lives. Have you noticed how the commercialization of products is being targeted to younger and younger age groups? Television commercials are directed to toddlers, with explicit instruction as to the type of diapers or pull-ups they should be wearing. With real babies featured in the commercials, simple words and catchy tunes to accompany them, the message is very convincing to the young and tender minds that see or hear them.

Throughout society, advertising impacts the way we live our lives. Magazines, television, radio, and the Internet survive through advertising. It is little wonder then that society has become bombarded with products and technology that are deemed essential. "Buy now, pay later" plans entice people who haven't the money to make enormous purchases *now* and not have to pay for a couple of years.

New housing developments call to readers through beautiful displays in weekend newspaper ads. They tell us how we should be living our lives: with a two-car garage, a bedroom for every child and more, multiple bathrooms, a family room, a large kitchen, dining, and living room, fireplace upstairs and down, etc., close to schools and community amenities. And the cost? This is also where the commercialization of society is directing the way we live our lives.

The cost, for most, requires more than one earner to be able to afford the home with the two-car garage and the lifestyle it suggests. It *is* affordable in many cases, however, with two salaries. So even when a young couple begins a family and wants to have one parent present in the home through the child's developing years, the reality—for most—in getting caught up in this commercially driven lifestyle is: *they can't.*

And the implications of both parents working are many. Extreme organization is required to be able to handle it all. The ongoing household needs within a large home are crucial. And if the young couple cannot afford to have someone assist with the household demands, they must reserve time and find the energy to do it themselves. There is always laundry to do and fold and put away, meals to cook, dishes to wash and put away, groceries to purchase and put away . . . homework to supervise . . . parent-teacher meetings to attend . . . clothing to buy for the whole family . . . extracurricular activities to organize for children also involving parental time . . . bills to pay . . . and on and on.

Somewhere in all of this, society also teaches that we need to find time for ourselves! And in the midst of everything listed above, this almost seems like a joke. How did life get to be like this? How did life get to be so hectic and out of control? Sadly also, many women tend to feel diminished if they don't have a job to go to outside the home.

Unfortunately, this is where many young people find themselves at the beginning of the third millennium. Snagged by the consumerism trap, they are succumbing to an over-consumption of unnecessary complications—rafts—in their lives. And in the process, they are burning out. Or they are divorcing because the stress of their lives has interfered with what might have been a good marriage for many. Stress has placed too much of a burden on the relationship, reducing the effectiveness of one or the other or both in being able to sustain their marriage vows or their initial commitment to one another.

The surge of anti-depressant drugs created to allow people to cope with life's stressors is most impressive. Equally impressive is the number of people using them. Prozac, for example, boasts that it is the most widely prescribed anti-depressant medication in history, having helped fifty-four million patients worldwide suffering from depression, obsessive-compulsive disorder, bulimia nervosa, and panic disorder.[17] This is only one of many drugs available to help those who are experiencing mental/emotional disorders. They have soared to the top of the insurable drug lists. Chemical imbalance is frequently quoted as the reason for the need for these drugs. Is it possible that the cause of this imbalance could be related to the way people are living their lives – with stress-induced reactions to unmet superhuman or commercially driven expectations from life?

People are often driven to succeed based on a popular belief that success is measured through one's financial status. It is this inner drive, then, that influences how they will live their lives, placing an inordinate value on the collection of "trophies" that money can buy. And further, technology plays right into the hands of the consumer by continually updating products with the most recently discovered capability, thus shortening the time between purchase and apparent obsolescence of expensive gadgetry. Gradually, lives fill up with these rafts—outdated technology—and the encumbrances they create, such as overspent credit cards with high interest rates on unpaid bills.

Is There Another Way?

Is there another way? Is there a way to simplify life? What is Sam and Elizabeth's secret?

If there is one thing I have found in my role of helping clients to become spiritually aware, it is this: as they open into spiritual awareness, they begin to de-clutter their lives. For some, this may mean a physical de-cluttering of their homes—culling their closets and drawers and then doing the same in their living space, getting rid of unnecessary furnishings, knick-knacks and outgrown toys, for example.

For others, de-cluttering means reconfiguring their lives and their life-style. They become very aware of the futility in which they race about each day, getting nowhere, and they begin to formulate plans to make serious lifestyle changes.

---

17 www.prozac.com, The Eli Lilly Company, 2006.

This may mean downsizing, for example, reducing the size of their homes or the number of hours they work each week. Or it could mean leaving or changing their jobs to find a more meaningful way to live their lives.

They may make a physical move to another location that imposes fewer demands or greater rewards; or they may decide to leave their spouse after many years of wanting to separate, no longer afraid to do so.

For some too, simplification is found through changes made in the activities of daily living. Dietary changes will be made that respect the nutritional needs of the individual and streamline their eating habits. They will use more natural products such as fresh fruits and vegetables, unrefined grains, etc., and reduce or stop their intake of processed foods that are high in salt, sugar, and food additives.

Many introduce regular, simple, and effective exercise into their lifestyle. They look at everything they do during the day to determine if they need to make any improvements, such as reducing the number of hours they spend in front of the television and spending more time with family and friends, or reading, or developing a creative hobby—something that will sustain them well into their later years—recognizing that the habits they form when they are young will follow them as they get older.

Whatever the changes, the spiritually aware person is beginning to simplify his life. He is beginning to welcome a new way of being into his life, and simplifying seems to be a big part of this change.

He is actually coming into conscious awareness of his need to simplify and to take advantage of his time spent within the physical dimension to do all that he can in the best way possible. Making his body and mind fit and receptive, through excellent food and regular exercise, is fundamental to this process.

A spiritually aware person also begins to develop a sense of gratitude that was not fully there previously. And with gratitude, comes an appreciation for everything he has—both personally and materially—and for everything he *is*. This kind of appreciation reduces the potential to get caught up in the societal portrayals of what one *needs* to be happy.

He is less vulnerable to fall prey to the commercialization of life. She doesn't need the big house to be happy. He doesn't need the latest in home theatre systems to be happy. They don't need a membership in the most elite country club to be happy. They appreciate what they have and no longer search for "something new" to make them feel better about their lives. They lose the sense that something is always missing. They find satisfaction in living with, and enjoying, what and whom they have in their lives.

This is not to say that a spiritually aware person begins to live her life as a hermit and gives up her possessions. A spiritually aware person wants to be comfortable. She wants to have a home that is set in an environment that makes her feel good. She wants to eat good food and she wants it prepared and served well.

The spiritually aware person sets high standards for himself. He just doesn't have a need for all of the superfluous things that obstruct his ability to connect with his own spirit and the life force within the universe. When his life is too demanding or too filled with technological toys, he is sidetracked from his mission of wanting connectedness with his spiritual nature. He forgets his spiritual nature.

The spiritually aware person wants to have fun also—the simple kind of fun that doesn't have a huge price tag associated with it. Simple family picnics at the beach by a lake, river, or ocean allow families to interact in play-related activities. Building sand castles together at any age, looking for seashells or special rocks, digging clams, or splashing one another in the water are all activities that children and parents both love once they are doing them. And these activities seem to make time stand still. They take parents and their kids out of the rush of life's Monday to Friday demanding routines. And they plant wonderful memories because of their sensual nature.

Playing board games as a family around the table on weekend evenings spells f-u-n for families, with laughter spilling over into the next day's happenings also. Going for family hikes on a Sunday afternoon while children are still young and anxious to spend time with Mom and Dad satisfy exercise and family interaction needs. All these simple activities teach children how to have simple fun so that they may continue to play and exercise as adults and to make play, exercise, and fun a priority in their lives always.

And none of these activities has anything to do with a television screen or a computer monitor—both of which are solitary activities, no matter how many people are in the room at the time. Generally speaking, they impede family interaction. Learning to interact with others and learning how to love one another begins in the home!

Playing together and having fun with your family, with each person feeling equal and important, is an enormously important foundation for well-being that every parent can give to his or her children. And it is a gift that will sustain children throughout their lives—a gift of healthy emotional maturity. As children become adults and marry and have children of their own, this gift will keep on giving as three generations continue to enjoy doing these simple things together.

And of course, the real message here is to take time out of busy schedules NOW to look at your life and to carve out some priorities—while you still can—that will influence how you are raising your children. As parents and grandparents, we automatically become role models for our children and grandchildren.

It is imperative that we seriously examine how we might be coming across to these most important young people in our lives. Are we so caught up in our own lives that we are missing out on opportunities to make a difference in the lives of those we love—regardless of our own age? Or do we make too many demands of our children—or too few—to allow them to grow up responsibly, in the security and understanding of the basics of love, kindness, and gratitude generously expressed and generously rewarded with even more loving kindness and grateful expression?

Simplify, Simplify, Simplify!

Have you ever felt "the rush" that comes from weeding clothes out of your clothes closet that you never wear and then putting them in bags for the Red Cross or some other benevolent organization?

Or, have you felt the invigoration that comes from relocating furniture in your home and, in the process, discover that some of it is hindering your living space as you find a "new home" for it somewhere else? Somehow after all of this change or reduction of furnishings, the energy in your home changes; it moves differently—better. The Chinese call this *feng shui*—the efficient and natural or unimpeded movement of positive energy flow throughout our homes or workspaces.

My mother had an expression that was obviously passed on down through the generations of her Irish ancestry that went something like this: *There is a place for everything and everything needs to be in its place*. Provided this expression is not interpreted to the level of perfectionist insanity, it holds a lot of merit for two reasons. First, when our homes are completely untidy, one wonders what state our minds are in. Is our cluttered living and workspace but a metaphor for our cluttered minds? And second, from a very practical point of view, and no doubt whence the expression arose, if there isn't enough space for the things you have accumulated, then perhaps you have accumulated too much!

Have you looked at your weekly/monthly schedule in full, lately? Have you considered reducing your commitments? Have you considered how you spend your day-to-day time with activities that no longer serve your expanding or changing needs? Is it time to reconfigure any of the things you are presently doing?

Just as our homes need a good spring cleaning each year with attention given to the way the energy moves within our homes, so, too, do our lives. The way in which we "spend" time in our lives needs a thorough examination. Because with each passing day, we are using up the time we have. One day it will all be used up. And when that day comes, we want to make sure that as we look back we are satisfied with the way we have used all the precious time we were given.

Happily, we don't have to wait until "that" day comes. We can do it now. And we can do it regularly. Just as successful business companies take time to evaluate their programs and services on a regular basis, we need to take time regularly to evaluate *what* we are doing and *how* we are doing it. What are we getting back for the energy we are investing?

And for those things we do in which we receive no positive feedback within ourselves, we need to be willing to either *stop* doing it or to find a *new way of doing it*—or to find a *new way of viewing it*. We need to bring *feng shui* into the tasks of our lives, as well as into the placement of the furnishings in our homes, to improve the positive energy flow throughout our lives.

Sometimes we just need to give ourselves a break from the busy routines of life, to ease up on some of our responsibilities—perceived or otherwise. Declare a sabbatical from committee work or from whatever activities seem to be zapping your energy. You will find that as a result of being out of the fray for awhile you will either miss the activity or you will feel relieved to be away from it.

Or, perhaps you need to take stock of it all and honestly face each facet of your life and make a decision—just as you would if you were going through your closets. "Does this suit me anymore? Is this the right colour for me now? Do I still enjoy wearing this?" And, as in the story at the beginning of this chapter about the man who built the raft, "Does this serve any purpose for me anymore?"

This symbolic way of looking at the things you do in your life will help you to make some decisions you may have been putting off for some time. And just as your closet is emptied of too many clothes and the air is able to circulate once again, so, too, is your own energy able to move once again when you have disengaged yourself from some of the activities that no longer hold meaning for you. The burden is instantly lifted when you leave the raft on the edge of the riverbank!

Simplifying your life goes beyond the physical activities you do. In taking stock, you also need to become aware of other energy-defeating things that create complication in your life as opposed to simplification. I am speaking of things like worry, fear, frustration, jealousy, regrets . . .

Each of these mental processes takes a toll on us. They deplete us of energy. They create tension within our bodies. In becoming spiritually aware, we begin to realize that we need to rid ourselves of these habits and behaviours. We need to *feng shui* our minds by completely cleaning out the debris that these behaviours create in us.

Simplifying our lives through the cessation of these behaviours and the release of the negative energies associated with them allows our bodies and our minds to begin to relax. We let go of the tension we hold in our bodies through worry and anger and regret. And as we rid ourselves of all the negative energy associated with these behaviours and the tension they create in us, we are able to move into an appreciation of the present.

We begin to live in the present—only the present. Here, our minds are quiet, uncluttered, and able to appreciate everything that is happening. Mental priority is no longer given to worry about the past or in planning every aspect of the future. Time is no longer spent fretting about what wasn't or what was. We become satisfied with the present and grateful and able to let go of our former way of being. And gradually, our minds give way, or *surrender*, to the spiritual guidance that has been trying to make itself known.

And through this simplification, we come to an acceptance of our lives and an acceptance of those who form the relationships in our lives. We begin to "tune in" to our body's natural rhythms and needs with a new awareness, and we respond to those rhythms and needs.

Having said all of this, life does bring unexpected demands that we sometimes have no choice but to meet—like losing a job and having to improve our education, or retrain, in order to seek new employment. At these times, life is not simple. This is the reality. It is essential, however, that modifications be made within our lives to acknowledge this new reality.

Even at stressful times, there are ways to simplify life. For example, some previous commitments may simply need to be placed on hold. And for those who have a family to support financially, the co-operation and emotional support of family in meeting this challenge will certainly help to reduce some of the stress. For despite the urgency to re-educate, one's family still remains the first priority. With full family support, the task is made easier. The burden is lightened.

I wish to say something also to those people who like to be "on the go" all of the time—the high achievers, who probably view my comments about simplifying life as a form of laziness, utter boredom, or something to be reserved for one's twilight years. There are times in one's life when opportunities are present to accomplish much, and to slow down at these times would seem unthinkable. But you still need to experience some form of downtime within these high-energy periods; otherwise, balance is lost. And worse: your perspective of the importance of your achievements is also lost. Downtime allows the high achiever some respite to become objective about what he is doing and to weigh his achievements against the demands he is placing upon himself and those with whom he shares his life. Without this downtime, he may become oblivious to the changing needs of his growing family, for example, or his life partner, or his aging parents, and the subsequent responsibility that falls to him in meeting these needs.

Finding Sabbath

And one final comment on the simplification of living has to do with something called *Sabbath*. This word comes from the Greek word *sabbaton* and the Hebrew word *shabbat*, meaning "to rest." In the Jewish tradition, the seventh day of the week was set aside to rest and receive spiritual enrichment, following God's example in Genesis 2: 3. Most Christians adopted Sunday to observe Sabbath, and although for centuries this day was kept as a day for attending church and doing restful activities, the meaning from which it was derived has been all but lost in Western civilization.

Sundays for most retail companies and sports businesses have become the same as any other day in cities throughout North America. And while one perception of this "24-7" routine of service provision may comfort the masses, we must also realize the price we pay for this relentless activity-charged world. We never slow down! We go, go, go, like a battery-operated toy, until we drop. And sometimes, by then it's too late.

Whether one comes from the Jewish and Christian traditions or not, there was great foresight in the observance of a day of rest once every week. To perceive a day of rest as just that—a day in which there is nothing challenging or with responsibility attached, and where one is able to rest and relax completely for the whole time—would a calmer and more peaceful world make! It slows everything down to a pace that allows for the drinking in of spiritual nourishment and of leisurely enjoyment of food and fellowship.

Instead, this gift of Sabbath is used by many as a day to get caught up—either at the office, or in the many jobs that have accumulated around one's home. We couldn't live without it because there are so many things to do! Consequently, in general our usage of Sabbath bears no resemblance to its original meaning and intent. Rest has nothing to do with it. It is simply a day away from one set of responsibilities to take on other responsibilities.

We can simplify our lives through the observance of Sabbath from the sense of rest and renewal. A full day of rest each week gives the body and the mind a chance to recuperate from the busy demands that are placed on both during the previous six days.

The knowledge that one day each week is going to be devoted to rest is, in itself, an amazing de-stressor! It offers light at the end of the tunnel. It serves to prevent individuals from burning out. It gives priority to self-preservation and teaches self-respectful ways of living in which we acknowledge the need to slow down and relax, to live healthy, full, and meaningful lives.

When we give ourselves this rest period, we give our bodies and minds a break from always performing—sometimes, at top speed—where there is little chance of ever feeling a sense of worship through the expression of gratitude for your life and for all that you are able to do.

In rest, we are renewed—restored to our original state. And in our original state, we do remember our spiritual self and the needs of our spirit. It is this that allows us to nourish our spirit in ways that will completely regenerate us. And then, we can begin a new week refreshed from the perceived burdens of life.

At this stage of simplification, we can enter a more contemplative lifestyle during the remainder of the week, where solace from a life epitomized by the words from the song at the top of this chapter can be found. Within a contemplative lifestyle, the frenetic running from one place to another finally stops. Time can be found to devote to reflection and stillness. Meditation sessions are successful and meaningful. The body, mind, and spirit connection is soothed and comforted—able to work its magic as a harmonic trio.

We move more slowly and purposefully. We are more observant of what is around us. We now see things that have always been there, which previously had eluded us because our thoughts were racing ahead of where we were or falling behind in reliving the past.

We may even drive our cars more slowly, no longer wanting the speed of the fast lane to alter the peaceful way we feel. And when we drive our cars within the speed limit, we are able to brake for butterflies and birds and animals when they come into our path. We see the wildflowers growing by the roadside and the beauty of all of nature's offerings. And we are filled with a sense of gratitude for being alive. We have gained control of our lives!

This type of simplification then allows us to live through the seasons of our lives with grace and thanksgiving. We are able to feel the pull of our natural instinctive being to withdraw from certain activities when it is time to do so. We rest when we need to rest. We engage again when we feel ready.

We respect and allow our body, mind, and spirit to live in wholeness—in harmony—and to experience a sense of self-respect, perhaps for the first time ever. We allow ourselves to see the beautiful spirit we really are—a loving spirit that is able to use its body and mind to accomplish whatever it needs to do, no longer hindered by the complexities of life.

Remaining Positive

All of this is part of the simplification of our lives. Life does not need to be difficult. We make it that way ourselves by the way in which we *choose to perceive* our lives and the way in which we *choose to respond* to the many situations that present themselves to us throughout our lives.

This does not mean that your life may never be without some form of tragedy. Events happen that are completely out of our control. Sometimes it feels so unfair that we are forced to find ourselves in situations that we would never choose for ourselves, but nonetheless we must find our way through the challenge. It is how we bring ourselves to these situations that dictates how we will meet the challenge.

To simplify one's life within a tragic situation is to bring to it the most positive mindset and the most positive outlook. This will not only help you, it will also help others who share your difficulties.

One need only look at the life of Christopher Reeve following his accident that left him as a quadriplegic, and at the lives of others less famous than Hollywood's Superman, to find inspiration to live through the most challenging of personal circumstances, tragedy, or loss.

The imprint that Terry Fox has left on Canadians is indelibly marked within our memories and permanently marked across Canada in multiple ways, in gratitude for his example in dealing with personal loss.

In fact, it is the depth of pain experienced through life's tragedies that somehow allows us to find our own ability to not only cope with this pain but to rise above it in some manner and to experience the height of life's pleasures as well. It is as though the degree to which we have experienced personal tragedy or loss somehow correlates with the degree to which we are capable of finding and experiencing pleasures like love and joy. And most certainly, anyone who has been healed of life's tragedies holds an enormous capacity to feel compassion for those who suffer in similar ways. It is in the deep expression of compassion that one is capable of truly exercising love and, therefore, experiencing the flow of divine energy.

The simplification of life does not suggest that you sit on the sidelines avoiding hard work or commitment. It means that for major activities you choose to engage in, you experience a sense of personal reward. Ideally, you will do them *with passion*.

Terry Fox was extremely passionate about his need to raise money for cancer research as he began his arduous run across Canada with only one leg. In other words, the activity—when it is right for you—will engage you in a positive energy flow throughout your being. Without this positive energy flow, Fox could never have faced the morning's chill, rain, or wind, or the pain of his daily run to meet his objective.

When passion is not present in your activities, it is time to reinvest your energies in something else that will once again create this positive energy flow. Or, it is time to view your obligations differently in an effort to create a renewed positive energy flow, or to summon some help with your obligations.

Are you passionate about what you do? Do you have any activity that you do that you are deeply passionate about? That sustains you? That seems to send you into a time warp where you just do not notice the passage of time, for you are so engaged in the activity and are enjoying every moment of it? This is what I mean by being passionate about something.

But passion must not be all consuming. When it is, life is no longer simple. It has become very complicated by virtue of the impact of your passion on the lives of those closest to you, if you are ignoring their needs.

When you are passionate about something, you are automatically engaged in the positive energy flow of your spirit. And by engaging in your passions, you are simplifying your life. Extraneous things will simply fall away, either because you don't really need them or haven't enough time, energy, or money for them. In other words, *you have enough* without these things.

"Would that there were an award for people who come to understand the concept of enough. Good enough. Successful enough. Thin enough. Rich enough. Socially responsible enough. When you have self respect," says Gail Sheehy, author of *Passages*,[18] "you have enough; and when you have enough, you have self-respect."

Simplify . . . Simplify . . . Simplify . . . How can you get to this way of being?

[18] Gail Sheehy, *Passages: Predictable Crises of Adult Life* (New York: Bantam Books, Inc., 1976), p. 513.

Take the time to discover yourself amidst whatever season of your life you are currently experiencing. Take the time *now* to get to know yourself at the level of your dynamic spiritual self. Take the time *now* to let your spiritual self introduce you to the exciting aspects of living a spiritually guided life.

And then, take the time to make the changes that your spirit will *insist* you make—that it will lovingly *guide* you to make—as you sprout your butterfly wings and transform into a new relationship with the divine aspect of your being, a part of *all that is.*

We people of earth have here the stuff of paradise,
We have enough.
We need no other stones to build the stairs on to the unfulfilled,
No other ivory for the doors, no other marble for the floors,
No other cedar for the beam and dome of man's immortal dream.
Here on the common human way is all the stuff to build a heaven;
Ours the stuff to build eternity in time.

Edwin Markham
(adapted)

TEN

THE WHOLE BODY, SACRED

If I could see in thee divinity, how would I treat thee?
If I could see in me divinity, how would I treat me?

Having reached the stage in one's spiritual evolution wherein we can envision ourselves as connected to the Divine Source of creation, it is time to look to the physical aspect of what makes us human—our bodies. And what easily flows from this is the obvious question: If our bodies have been divinely created, *are they sacred?*

As a former volunteer on the pastoral perinatal bereavement team in my local hospital, the word *sacred* was used to describe the miniature body of the aborted fetus. In fact, it was because this word was used in conjunction with the mandate of the program—to help parents cope with their grief—that I agreed to serve in such an emotionally challenging aspect of end-of-life care. "Sacred" is a word we do not use or hear very often outside of religious discussion. It is a word that causes us to stop and think.

If we were to allow ourselves to perceive our physical bodies as sacred, it would change many of our views about ourselves. It would make us want to take very good care of our physical bodies. Like the sacred body of the deceased infant, we would carefully and tenderly treat our body with the respect it deserves. We would bring tenderness and respect to it as we clean it and pat it dry carefully, applying creams, lotions or powders that are suitable for our skin. We would dress it in clean and well-kept clothes made from fabrics that allow our skin to breathe and experience comfort as our bodies move with ease.

Learning to treat our bodies in a caring manner lets us experience the divine within our bodies. It brings our attention into slow motion as we encounter our daily ablutions of self-care, after which we give thanks for the body we are privileged to live within.

In my earlier book, *energywellness.ca*, I devoted a chapter to the many ways of caring for our physical bodies through excellent nutrition, regular exercise, adequate sleep, etc. These same topics need to be revisited through the lens of the word *sacred* in conjunction with the whole body. If your body has been neglected through lack of exercise and good nutrition, then your attention given to these most important areas at this time will serve to alter your perception about your body and allow you to understand its sacred and beautiful quality.

The Body Beautiful

Western society is obsessed with images of beautiful bodies of both men and women. In these images, the women are always thin and shapely; the men are muscular and tight; neither has any fat bulging out anywhere. With daily exposure to these images, we begin to believe we should look like the models who portray them. We see them on television commercials and programming, in magazine ads, in movies, in posters on our buses, and so on. To maintain these model figures, women must eat less than the average number of calories for their age group or be extremely active and burn all the additional calories they consume. So for most, it simply isn't practical or realistic to try to emulate the pictures we are faced with every day.

Also, the reality is that we were not all given to the same "ideal" body shapes—and isn't this wonderful, for what a dull world it would be if everyone looked the same. At the same time, however, obesity has never been so pronounced as it is now. It is a reflection of a sedentary lifestyle combined with an inundation of fast, processed foods that are high in fat, sugar, salt, and unnatural food additives. Being overweight doesn't feel good, it doesn't look good, and it simply isn't healthy!

What is both practical, realistic, and healthy is a diet that is rich in high-fibre foods of fresh fruits and vegetables, legumes and whole grains; adequate in protein, monounsaturated fat and water; and low in animal fat, sugar, processed foods, caffeinated or sweet beverages. When combined with daily exercise, this formula for daily living will not only make you feel well, it will allow your body to find its natural body weight, where it will remain with little effort for most of your life.

Here, regardless of your body shape, you may feel comfortable in your clothes and confident in your appearance, and—most important—you can begin to love your body. When you cannot love your body, it becomes a difficult task to love what is inside your body—your spirit. This is such an important step in engaging in one's spiritual journey! The sacred body wants to find balance in terms of ideal weight so that it can function at its best level of performance for us.

We need to understand this simple yet crucial point and address it every day for the *rest of our lives*. In this way, we acknowledge the sacred body we live within and we bring honour to it through the quality and amount of food we offer it and in the exercise we encourage it to carry out. To do otherwise is to deny it what it needs for top performance. And we are the ones who will suffer from making unwise and unhealthy choices.

Sacred Sensuality

Let's take a look now at some other aspects of the sacred body. We'll begin with our senses. Five of the most precious gifts of our divine creation are our senses. And as with the intention in all gifts, our senses are meant to be used fully, every day. And we *do* use them. But do we use them fully? Do we take the time to really see what it is throughout nature and throughout our own life that connects us to the divine within creation? Do we truly *hear* and *listen to* what others are saying to us, in both words and actions?

Do we take time each day to experience a heartfelt feeling of gratitude for the sacred gifts of our sight . . . our hearing . . . our ability to smell and to taste beautiful foods . . . and our ability to touch? Or, like so many of our divine gifts, do we take them for granted? And what about our "sixth sense"? Do we allow our intuition to be heard, interpreted, and used, or do we slough it off as irrelevant?

The Sacred Gift of Communion

Do we engage our senses within the context of their *sacred* quality? It is from the sacred that we are able to enter into truly meaningful relationship with others, where we see the positive rather than the negative and where we build on one another's positive attributes. This is where we slip into intuitive communion with one another and allow the opportunity for the divine and sacred expression of our spirit to flow through us and into the other.

We have been given the gift of verbal communication as a result of exquisitely formed tissue of the larynx that incredibly allows us to make sound that is *unique* to us. We are meant to commune with one another, otherwise we wouldn't have been given such elaborate, divinely created tools to do this!

We are meant to commune with one another in so many ways to experience the full range of our positive emotions with others, all of which are gifts from our spirit. For when we engage in positive emotion of any kind, we automatically connect with the positive energy flow of our spirit and stimulate the same in others.

One of the main purposes of human communion is to give of ourselves, particularly in fertile areas where our willingness to share ourselves with others is well received. We do this through kindness and consideration of and for others at all times, often putting others' needs before our own.

We commune by willingly sharing what we have with others who have less. And in the giving of ourselves to these situations, we always receive back . . . sometimes more than we have given. This is all part of our human divinity, the communion of our spirit. What we receive back may not be of the same *nature* as what we shared, but it will be something that meets our own special needs. And it may not come from the place to which we gave our energy. It may simply fall into the category of abundance that is present within our life. And the more grateful we are for our abundance, the more abundance we will experience.

We also commune in light or serious conversation. We commune in the private intimacy of a sexual relationship with our life partner. We commune as a sharing member of our family unit and as a responsible member within our community in a variety of ways. We commune as a team member in a work setting or in an organized sport such as relay, baseball, soccer, hockey, curling . . .

We have been given the ability to converse through speech and through nonverbal behaviours. To not use these abilities in the way they were intended is to not fully engage our whole body and mind and, therefore, to not fully engage our spirit.

The Sacred Body and Mind

Beyond these gifts of our senses and of communication, we have been given limbs to use, to function in so many ways, with all of our muscles working in complete harmony with one another when we use our bodies with respect. The functioning of the healthy human body and mind is an amazing study. It fills us with awe as we stop to truly appreciate the power of the human body and mind.

We are meant to commune using *all* of our gifts: our senses, our intelligence, our whole body's and mind's many abilities . . . and our talents. Combined, they allow us to come fully into communion and relationship with others and to maintain a balance in living. It is this balance that enables us to experience the divine in all that we do, and to allow this quality or way of being into our relationships with others.

When we do not use our gifts, abilities, and talents or when we overuse some and neglect others, we very quickly go out of what we know as *balanced living*. To restore this balance, we need to review all that we are doing and not doing and begin to make changes that are essential to respect the sacred quality of our human potential.

Our body and mind need the combination of *all* our sensory qualities, along with the full use of our intelligence, abilities and talents to free our spirit and allow divinity to flow through us. *Our spirit thrives in us through our full expression of our human potential.* And to the degree to which we do not reach our potential, we correspondingly thwart our spirit's ability to fulfill its evolving purpose in this lifetime.

Purpose is not static; it is evolutionary. Whereas we may feel completely in tune with our spiritual purpose at some point in life, we cannot rest there, thinking that this was all we have been called to do. *As long as our spirit breathes life into our bodies, our lives are meant to remain filled with evolving purpose and continuing potential.*

So pay attention to all the signs your body, mind, emotions, and spirit are attempting to have translated into your awareness and incumbent action. The physical body speaks to us in very loud tones sometimes, not only in fatigue and pain from overuse, but also from physical weariness or the fatigue of underuse. Our bodies are meant to be used. They are meant to be exercised adequately so they may remain strong and able. Our minds speak to us also, from overuse and underuse.

As we learn to understand the language of our own unique body, we learn to respect what it is attempting to tell us through the particular symptom(s) it is reflecting to us. And from there, we can take the necessary action required to address the specific symptom(s) adequately.

A bout of intense illness may even enlighten us to a new way of being wherein we truly understand the *sacred quality* of our whole body and mind—its meaning for us personally and its influence throughout humanity and the natural world.

By listening, understanding, and respecting the needs of our body, mind, and spirit, we can sometimes stave off the need for medical attention—possibly arresting a condition that might have developed into something more serious. Herein, we are respecting the divine reality of our existence—that we *do* possess an inner sense of knowing when something is wrong, and that our bodies have an innate ability to heal themselves when given a chance to do so.

The key to early, self-corrective healing is learning to respond *immediately* to the signs the body *and* mind *and* spirit are reflecting and take them into prayer or meditation that we might be shown what to do. This is not to say that we do not need to seek medical advice. It is only to suggest that by becoming aware of the signs our bodies and minds are reflecting to us, we may be able to correspondingly respond in the manner they are asking of us and change something we are doing or incorporate new activities—either or both of which may bring solace or healing.

The Sacred Gift of Emotions

And finally, we have been given the gift of emotions. Emotions work with the body and the mind to allow us to express ourselves fully. They assist us as we enter into communion with one another. In this sense, they are part of our *sacred self* that forms our humanity. They help us to find an essential balance in living. Combined with the physical sensations that arise from the body, our emotions allow us to feel *in* complete balance or completely *out* of balance.

Balanced living means that our body is sufficiently challenged and rested, our mind is sufficiently challenged and rested, and our emotions comfortably allow us to feel good within our body and mind. When the body and mind are thus in harmony, the spirit is able to flourish.

On the other hand, if our body suffers from exhaustion due to overuse or underuse, our emotions allow our minds to experience a sense of being out of balance. We will be more vulnerable to outbursts of anger, frustration, impatience, or even "the blues." In a simple scenario of the underused body, going for a walk outdoors will help the body and mind to feel better. And for the overused body, a good night's sleep will not only help the body to recover its lost energy, it will also soothe the emotions that worked with the physical symptom of fatigue to make one feel better emotionally as well.

Emotions are integral to both the body and the mind since they are connected physically and mentally to one's being, causing physiological change as they are experienced. If emotions are negative, therefore, they impact the body and mind in a negative way, temporarily stopping the positive flow of spiritual energy into one's being. But if they are positive, they only strengthen the body and mind and contribute to a sense of well-being and wholeness.

Emotions are also like gifts of the spirit and in that sense they may be considered *sacred* when we understand their relevance to our overall sense of wholeness. Clearly, negative emotion does not feel good when it is held inside, nor does it translate well to others when we experience it in their company. And anything that cuts us off from a feeling of wholeness has negative implications for us.

With awareness of oneself as a spiritual being, we recognize that the expression of negative emotion holds a deeper meaning and understanding for us. It is a form of spiritual distress alerting us that we have perhaps strayed too far from our original way of being—our spiritual nature—and we must find a way to return.

We are like a lost sheep separated from its flock. We need to be able to hear the familiar and trusted voice of our inner "good shepherd" to help us find the safe road home to our spiritual nature once again. For it is here that we find both completeness as a part of the flock and wholeness within ourselves. Indeed, it is this aspect of completeness arising from our human need to commune with others in positive ways that contributes to a feeling of wholeness within the self.

Are our emotions the voice of our spirit? Or are our emotions *messages* from our spirit? The former interpretation is often the one that is assumed. "Her spirits were low," is sometimes heard as a remark; or, "Getting out of the house will raise your spirits!"

Let's look at the second interpretation, that our emotions are *messages from our spirit*. Given the wide range of emotions we humans possess, our emotions *are* like messages from the spirit in the sense that they are an indicator of how "connected" we are with the positive energy flow of our spirit. And, depending upon the particular emotion that is being expressed, our spirit informs us—through our feelings—whether we are connected or disconnected from our spirit by virtue of the type of energy that is generated by the emotion.

As explained in depth in chapter six, our spirit is constantly fuelled by divine love, which is always available to us. Despite this, we interrupt our ability to experience this positive energy flow each time we engage in unloving behaviour or thoughts about ourselves or of someone else. By moving into an unloving state, we effectively cut ourselves off—temporarily—from the positive energy flow of our spirit. We experience this feeling of being cut off as negative emotion accompanied by its side-effects of lethargy, apathy, fatigue, etc., to name only a few.

Our mind is in control of this part of our being—the cutting off from the spirit—by focusing on the negative. In the case of an under-challenged mind, for example, the mind has all sorts of time and opportunity to focus on those things that make a person feel "less than" or "better than" and soon one is caught up in a negative or inauthentic place within—the place that spurs and reinforces this way of being.

The most distressing symptom of being cut off from one's spiritual Source is depression. But depression need not be seen as an end result of many things having gone wrong. Instead, let it be viewed as a loud *message from the spirit* that there is another way of living that invokes your spirit to provide essential guidance. In this way of being, the mind takes on a drug-free and supportive role of carrying out the direction of the spirit.

It is the mind—as wonderfully formed and amazingly able as it is—that keeps us locked up in our own self-created prisons, removing us from a place of love and capable of bringing us dangerously close to the edges of mental or physical illness. No one needs to go through life locked up in the negative places of her mind. No one! Finding one's spirit is the key to open the door of the prison that may be within.

The mind must be considered *sacred* also, since it has been divinely created. And regardless of what has happened in a person's past, the healthy mind has the capacity to understand that it needs to open to the spirit and allow it to surface, to be experienced and heard.

The Sacred Act of Surrender

It is the sacred act of *surrendering* to one's spirit for guidance that erases all evidence of mental prisons from the past. One's positive spiritual energy can now flow, uninterrupted. The body and mind absorb this constant spiritual energy flow as the dynamic of love and inner peace. It is this that positions its host to hold others within the same positive energy embrace.

But it isn't easy to do this . . . to surrender completely. It may take many attempts plus self-reminders and affirmations to completely let go of the notion that you must always be "in control" of your life. According to author Carolyn Myss, the idea of releasing one's power of choice to a Divine Force remains the greatest struggle for the individual seeking to become conscious.[19]

---

[19] Caroline Myss, Ph.D., *Anatomy of the Spirit: The Seven Stages of Power and Healing* (New York: Three Rivers Press, 1996), p. 220.

From a very practical viewpoint, it isn't easy to surrender, particularly when we have lived a life of taking charge of our daily activities. Surrendering to a force that we cannot see seems completely foreign to us, and certainly not associated with a choice that we would sensibly make living in a "high-tech," scientifically driven age.

We need to be reminded again of the good shepherd, whose voice is the only one his sheep recognize and are willing to follow.[20] And because of this they are willing to put complete trust in this voice and be led where the voice takes them.

Listening to the voice of our spirit is the same. We first need to be able to hear it, however, and to acknowledge that it is indeed the voice of our spirit, before we can respond to its promptings.

To release our power of choice and to surrender to the Divine, we need to perceive ourselves as body, mind, *and* spirit. Otherwise, our perception of *self* is that of a one-dimensional being that lives for a time and eventually dies. There is no continuum of spirit in this myopic interpretation of life.

We are multi-dimensional beings! We contain intelligence within our physical body as well as our mind. We also contain a wealth of intelligence and wisdom in the spiritual aspect of our being in our soul. The power of surrender engages us in an exciting awareness of the various voices we contain in our being—in our body, our mind, and our spirit.

Spiritual Distress . . . the Inability to Surrender

Ask yourself the next time you have a physical symptom that occurs anywhere in your body: *What is my body trying to tell me*? And then, try to understand exactly what your body is telling you. Is it simply a matter of overextending yourself physically and not allowing sufficient time for your body to recover and get all of the rest it needs to meet the demands you place on it?

Or is your body attempting to speak to you more directly by resisting certain expectations you are placing on it? Are you engaging in any behaviour that your body is resisting? If the body contains intelligence within its cells, then it is plausible that your body may react in ways to defend itself against some of the activities you engage in through the inharmonious use of your mental processes.

Resistance may be experienced as undesirable physical symptoms. If you were to translate any of these symptoms using the voice of your spirit and then reverse the demand you had placed on your body by your mind, quite possibly the undesirable physical symptoms would disappear.

As an example, there could be a person in your life that your body and mind are rejecting, expressing this rejection in bodily symptoms long before

---

20 John 10: 3-4, 14.

your mind consciously acknowledges the need to either move away from this person or to change the way you relate to him or her. Or it may be a behaviour that you have indulged in reluctantly that has negatively impacted the way you feel physically and emotionally. Or it might be the work you are paid to do that no longer feels right for you. Or you may feel responsible for someone else's well-being—which is completely out of your control—and experience emotionally based physical symptoms related to your inability to control or effect change in this person.

Or perhaps you are feeding your sacred body foods that are not aligned with its changing needs. The move to a vegetarian lifestyle, for example, is a journey of self-discovery wherein one learns to listen to the sacred body's changing needs and subsequent rejection of meat, animal fat, and all foods associated with animal products. As well, many people find they are lactose intolerant as they grow older. Their bodies are rejecting the milk-related foods they are being fed.

By not listening to and acknowledging the sacred body's changing needs, the subsequent physical symptoms that ensue may be interpreted as spiritual distress—the inability to take direction from your spirit rather than from your mind. Retraining your mind to allow you to hear the good shepherd in your spirit's voice requires that you engage in many activities that will lure your spirit out so it may be activated in all that you do. The mind needs to be trained to listen to the spirit's voice—the good shepherd—to do this.

The appreciation of nature, listening to meaningful music, engaging in moments of meditation, self-directed prayer, an awareness of the need to let go, cleansing journalling, energy healing, physical exercise, excellent nutrition and adequate sleep, living in a clean, comfortable, and "feel-good" environment, using colours that are compatible with who you are and that suit your evolving needs, etc., in concert with care and consideration of and for others, all help to heal the sacred mind and body of their emotional scars and allow the opening for a spiritually guided life to become possible.

When our bodies are viewed as sacred and our spirit's voice has been acknowledged, there is no more need for artificial stimulants like cigarettes and alcohol, street drugs, drugs in sports, indefinite use of antidepressants, etc. Instead, people will be "hooked" on their spirituality. They will have found the continuous link to the pleasures available *within* their bodies, in their own spirit and soul. This is the only "high" they will need.

And when they are on this "trip," they will not only be safe to drive, or "clean" to compete, they will be capable of doing their absolute best in all they do, whether it is training to become an Olympic athlete, managing a business, being a stay-at-home mom, or aging gracefully. They will be in touch with *their absolute best* and able to derive all the pleasure, strength, endurance, and energy that come from this. And *this* will be their true gift to the world—their absolute best!

The whole body is sacred. As we understand that this *is* so and begin to view our own bodies and those of others as sacred, we approach our spiritual potential within our human expression. We offer ourselves to have the work of the Divine Source of Creation happen through us—a partnership based on the divinity we share with the universe—as we fulfill our mission within humanity. We see ourselves in *all that is* and we see all that is within ourselves.

. . . the kingdom of God is within you.

Luke 17:21

Epilogue

Enter through the narrow gate; for the gate is wide and the way is broad that leads to destruction, and there are many who enter through it. For the gate is small and the way is narrow that leads to life, and there are few who find it.

Matthew 7:13, 14

We cannot be *in* all that is without having the Divine energy of God *in us*. Stated another way, we cannot be in all that is without being a part of the universal life force, the energy of creation—*the kingdom of God*. It is this energy that links all living things and that is within all living things. It is this energy that transfers prayer and distant healing intention between persons throughout the world.

We tap into this energy through our intention and the awareness that we possess the ability to do so. All we need to do is *will* it to be, and our healing or prayerful thoughts are instantly transferred to the person who is on our mind—faster than the highest-speed Internet connection!

Our positive intention becomes part of the positive energy within the universal life force, the energy that is always available to flow into us. It is amplified for us when someone intentionally thinks positively about us or prays for us. When we are "open" to receive this amplification of energy, we are positively affected by it.

Prayer lines or circles for the sick are very effective for this reason. The number of people praying increases the receiving person's positive energy flow, and he is inundated with healing energy. And here, the recipient finds renewed inner strength either to take him through his healing process or to face the reality of his condition and be comforted.

When we tap into this *God-force* within our own being with healing or prayerful intention for others, we are effectively using this divine energy like a telephone line that transmits a message to someone. The healing energy is not coming from some entity that is "out there," somewhere distant. It is coming from *within us* through our intention to assist someone else through whatever difficulty that has occurred in her life.

And like an instant flash, this healing intention is transferred immediately to the person in our thoughts, amplifying the capacity for her own positive energy to flow throughout her being. *It is our spiritual connection to the God-force that allows this to happen*. This is the amazing potential of the divinity of man. We all possess the ability to do this—to impact others in positive ways through our healing intention to do so.

I am not suggesting that there isn't a more profound intensity of energy within the universe that is infinitely greater than that which we hold within our own human selves. And further, I am not suggesting that anyone can ever truly understand the concept or *mystery* of God, *the Universe*, or a higher intelligence.

What I am saying is that because we are spiritual beings living in the human dimension, we all contain the potential for the God-force or Buddha-nature to be fully activated within our being that divinity may flow through us. It is this that connects us to one another. It is this energy connection, then, that allows divinity to be found in the simplest of situations.

It is this *Divine* energy connection that allows us to serve others in Divine ways, as "servants of God." As *servants*, we are simply falling into the ways of a Divine energy connection and taking our guidance from this Divine part of our spiritual nature. And further, it is this Divine energy connection that links us to *all that is*. *We are entering through the narrow gate and finding life.*

If any of what I am saying in this book is correct, then one must ask: Why is it that people do not always behave in Divine ways with one another? What is it that keeps people from seeing themselves in *all that is*? If people truly hold Divine energy within themselves, why isn't the world a more peaceful place? Why do so many people enter through the wide gate that leads to destruction?

Regrettably, in general, we have forgotten our spiritual nature. And because of this, we lose faith with our fellow man in many ways because of what we constantly do to one another as physical beings. Therefore, it seems virtually ridiculous to think of humanity as having *divine* qualities or potential.

It is so much more realistic to think only in terms of divinity as being associated with a *Godhead*. This is safe. *God* is in *His* heaven, and we are here on earth, and in that scenario, everything makes sense.

We may believe that our image of "God" has divine power to part the waters and turn the tides, etc. And we may want to embrace the understanding that this divine power is something we can call upon when we are in need.

It would, therefore, be unthinkable to see divinity as being *associated with people* who form relationships within our lives and who presumably are *disassociated with power*. And so we close ourselves off from this kind of "possibility thinking."

Furthermore, when this is the traditional mindset of the majority of believers in God or *a Supreme Being*, it becomes impossible to think in terms of *being in all that is*. It simply makes no sense. There is no logic to it, no link to any other relevant piece of information to allow such a concept to take on meaning and be credible.

So we continue to act in ways that separate us from feeling a part of being in all that is. We continue to dishonour one another, to withhold the truth, and to cover up our errors in judgment. We continue to accrue bad feelings about others. We continue to destroy the environment. We continue to take more than we need. We continue to put our needs before the needs of others.

And yet, all the while, many of us claim a belief in *God* or in a *Divine Being*. And to this *Divine Being* we continue to go for absolution of our errors in judgment, our lies, and our selfish and disrespectful behaviours. Despite the degree of offence we may have caused others, it seems that as long as we take it to a Divine, Supreme Being for forgiveness, all is made well again for us.

But what about the person(s) who has had to suffer the effects of our behaviour? Their suffering is obliterated within our own selfish supplication for mercy. This is but one way in which our global society has not evolved as a species on this planet.

Technologically, we have been able to split the atom, we have been able to put people on the moon, and more, but we have not yet learned how to love one another.

And we will never love one another until we learn to love ourselves! For the effect of acting in ways that dishonour someone else is also felt within the self, in the soul. It is felt as negative energy that is out of alignment with our natural energy flow—despite the forgiveness we may believe we have received by way of confession. And if we are unaware of our own spirituality, we remain unaware of the effect of this negative energy that we continually accrue.

The way to change the world and create peace is to love one another. And this means that first we must love ourselves! We will never love ourselves while we continue to lie, to dishonour others, and to act in selfish ways.

And we will never be able to love ourselves unconditionally until we heal that which has made us not love ourselves. This takes us right back to the beginning again and the need to become aware of all those areas in ourselves that are out of balance.

The way to change the world is to first change the way you yourself behave. And to change your own ways, you need to become aware of what is not in alignment with a positive energy flow—the stuff that *can* change the world.

As you develop the conscious awareness of yourself as a spiritual being, and face the aspects of your humanity that no longer serve your spiritual nature, you will come into a new way of being. In this place, you will be free of self-righteous attitudes and behaviour; you *will* find love—unconditional love—for yourself and for others.

You *will* find respect for yourself and others. There will be no more need for lies or disrespectful and selfish behaviours. And because you will begin to care more for yourself (in a non-egocentric way) *and* others, you will begin to tap into the positive energy flow that runs between the lives of those you love and between you and the lives of people you do not know and will never know.

You will begin to see yourself as being connected to these people through your spiritual commonality. Your focus will become the commonality of the human condition as opposed to the separateness of it.

All you have to do is to willingly and mindfully open yourself into this new way of thinking. This will allow you to cross the invisible boundary of your mind (to pass through the narrow gate) and enter the quiet, beautiful and sacred space of your divine inner spirit. And with the power of your intention to find it, you will.

And from this new place of reality and sense of connectedness, the potential of seeing yourself in others and them in you becomes less of a mystery. The potential of seeing yourself in *all that is* becomes possible.

Making a connection with one's own spirit allows people to move through their dark night, given the realization that there is something else in life besides what they have been living, something that will bring them meaning and sustenance.

The knowledge that we are spirit that is connected to something much greater than ourselves alone gives hope to those who suffer unthinkable tragedy. It provides assurance to those who are about to embark upon a new pathway on their journey of life. It offers courage to those who must go into battle for their country and possibly endure an untimely death. It gives confidence to those who are faced with lesser challenges also, like writing an exam or starting a new job or taking a driving test.

Human spirituality provides the strength to face the reality of a disabling or terminal illness. By serving as a connector to the Source of creation, it opens the door to seeing one's human life as a short stopover on his spiritual journey throughout eternity. It allows the knowing mind of the dying body to melt into the comfort and security of something much greater within the spiritual dimension to which he is already attached. One's human life, in years, is but a pause between sentences in the spiritual dimension. With the death of the physical body, the conversation of its departed spirit quietly continues where it left off less than a blink ago.

Human spirituality allows you to feel a new and exciting dimension of your life—a dimension you cannot see but you can *feel*. And the more you can focus on *this* dimension, the more you can begin to live a *balanced* life from the knowledge that you *are* more than your physical body; for this seems to be the biggest stumbling block for anyone from accepting his or her own spirituality. They cannot *see* it.

Understanding that *you can feel it* and understanding *how* you feel it and how it can guide you in your life—because of its connection to universal life energy—opens you into the greatest networking opportunity ever to be given to you.

The final prescription I leave with you for healing your life then, is: *Learn to embrace your spiritual self through whatever way is meaningful for you.* Understand that your spirit is always with you wherever you go, wherever you are, in life and in death. Death is not the end. Rather, death is simply a transition into *another way of being in spirit*. It is not something to be feared, therefore, nor is it something to rush towards.

Physical life affords wondrous opportunities for the spirit to experience the physical reality and dimension of life. To purposely shorten one's time on earth or to waste one's time on earth is to abort this spiritual opportunity. It suggests a complete lack of understanding, awareness, and respect of oneself as a spiritual being. Furthermore, it suggests a lack of understanding of oneself as a spiritual being on a human adventure—able to experience all of the emotions and sensations that accompany the physical reality. It disempowers and discredits one's ability to heal and restore oneself to purposeful living, wherein one's spirit is free to explore everything it wants to explore during the brief time it is in this physical reality.

Without understanding oneself as a spiritual being, it is impossible to fully appreciate oneself as a physical being. And it is impossible to understand the interdependent relationship that exists between the body, the mind, and the spirit, as it relates to one's health and well-being.

Religions that neither acknowledge nor emphasize this in their teachings serve to hold us in the dark rather than leading us into the light. They hold their believers in the physical and lowest aspect of their human evolution and prevent them from experiencing the unlimited potential their physical life can offer them through an awakened spirit.

And as a last word, it is becoming clear to me that as we open ourselves to the divinity in our being, we correspondingly open ourselves to *all* the possibilities that are so available to us within divinity. The song that says, "Love is nothing till you give it away, then it comes right back to you" exemplifies this concept very well. *It is only when we are able to acknowledge the energies of divinity that we are able to experience their value.* The more we acknowledge this, the more deeply we open ourselves to the divinity within creation, and thus within ourselves.

What this means is that we are able to derive more and more pleasure out of life. We are able to experience life and the incredible design within the divinity of creation that allows us to appreciate beauty, to love to the fullest, to feel joy as a moment-to-moment ingredient of our life, and to be filled with the peace that comes from these qualities. This is our birthright! These are the energies within creation that are free for the taking by all who wish to find them! They cannot be found in the presence of control, judgment, or any of the common negative qualities that are found throughout mankind. It is only in the relinquishing of these negative qualities that we find the peace for which we so desperately search!

The more we align with divine energy, the more we experience this positive energy in all aspects of our lives—in all our relationships; in our unlimited capacity to give and receive love; in our ability to appreciate beauty in all that is—and thus to be filled with the joy and the powerful effect of the Holy Spirit working within us.

Divine energy is always available, always waiting to be embraced by you, for it is always embracing you.[21] By learning to embrace your spirit during your life—through whatever way is meaningful for you—you will be led into the *spiritual dimension of your physical reality*. Here, you will be able to comprehend that not only are you a part of all that is; in fact, you are *in* all that is, and *all that is*, is also in you.

I am in you and you are in me!
Together we engage in this journey.
We are each a part of Divinity.
We are in all that is.

Judith

21 Judith M. Campbell, *energywellness.ca* (Renfrew, Ont: General Store Publishing House, 2004).

About the Author

Judith M. Campbell is a Wellness Consultant with over thirty years' experience in community and occupational health nursing, fifteen of which were served at a senior management level. She began her journey as an energy worker in 1993. Since retiring from active nursing service, she has added the teaching of body, mind, and spirit awareness courses, workshops, and retreats to her energy-healing practice.

She started her writing career shortly after retiring. Her first book, *energywellness.ca*, was published in 2004. Since that time, she has begun a series of children's books on the subject of body, mind, and spirit awareness, called *Joey Wholeness*.

She is a lover of nature, a walker, singer, curler, and yoga enthusiast and is devoted to her family. Her life's journey has quite naturally led her on her own spiritual quest, which has culminated in a deep understanding and respect for the spiritual dimension within humanity and throughout creation. It is this understanding that she most wishes to convey to others through her creative writing and teaching.

She shares her love for life, family, and friends with her best friend, husband, and teacher, David.